Contents

Preface   v

Section One:
Relating to Nature
Things That Grow: *Gomasuri* □ *Hana ni Ara*
□ *Hana yori Dango* □ *Imo [no Ko] o Arau Yoo*
□ *Iwanu ga Hana* □ *Korogaru Ishi ni Koke Mus*
□ *Minoru hodo Atama no Sagaru Inaho Kana*
□ *Nemawashi* □ *Ne mo Ha mo Nai* □ *Sakura*
□ *Sanshoo wa Kotsubu de mo [Piririto] Karai* □ *Takane
no Hana* □ *Take o Watta Yoo* □ *Uri Futatsu* □ *Yoraba
Taiju no Kage*
Water, Wind, and Clouds: *Ame ga Furoo to Yari
ga Furoo to* □ *Ame Futte Ji Katamaru* □ *Kaze no
Tayori* □ *Kumo o Tsukamu Yoo* □ *Mizu ni Nagasu*
□ *Mizu no Awa* □ *Mizu o Utta Yoo* □ *Mizu Shoobai*
□ *Yakeishi ni Mizu*

Section Two: Idioms
Creatures Large and Small   **25–46**
Birds and Beasts: *Ashimoto kara Tori ga Tatsu*
□ *Hane o Nobasu* □ *Karite Kita Neko no Yoo* □ *Neko
mo Shakushi mo* □ *Neko ni Koban* □ *Neko no Hitai*
□ *Neko no Te mo Karitai* □ *Onaji Ana no Mujina*
□ *Suzume no Namida* □ *Tatsu Tori Ato o Nigosazu*
□ *Tsuru no Hitokoe* □ *Uma no Hone*
Fish, Frogs, and Others: *Gomame no Hagishiri*
□ *Hachi no Su o Tsutsuita Yoo* □ *Hippari Dako* □ *I no
Naka no Kawazu [Taikai o Shirazu]* □ *Ka no Naku
Yoona Koe* □ *Manaita no Ue no Koi* □ *Mushi no Iki*
□ *Nakitsura ni Hachi* □ *Saba o Yomu* □ *Tade Kuu
Mushi mo Sukizuki*

Section Three: Idioms
The Human Body   **47–65**
Abata mo Ekubo □ *Agura o Kaku* □ *Ashimoto o Miru*

KT-417-551

□ *Ashi o Arau* □ *Atama ga Sagaru* □ *Awaseru Kao ga Nai* □ *Haragei* □ *Ishin Denshin* □ *Kao ga Hiroi* □ *Katami ga Semai* □ *Koshi ga Hikui* □ *Mimi ga Itai* □ *Ryooyaku Kuchi ni Nigashi* □ *Shinzoo ga Tsuyoi* □ *Shiroi Me de Miru* □ *Tsura no Kawa ga Atsui* □ *Ude o Migaku* □ *Ushirogami o Hikareru Omoi* □ *Ushiroyubi o Sasareru Yoo*

Section Four: Idioms
From One to Ten and More   **66–76**

Chiri mo Tsumoreba Yama to Naru □ *Happoo Bijin* □ *Hito Hata Ageru* □ *Hitori Zumoo o Toru* □ *Ishi no Ue ni mo Sannen* □ *Juunin Toiro* □ *Nimaijita o Tsukau* □ *Ni no Ashi o Fumu* □ *Onna Sannin Yoreba Kashimashii* □ *Sannin Yoreba Monju no Chie* □ *Sushizume*

Section Five: Idioms
From Place to Place   **77–82**

Ana ga Attara Hairitai □ *Ishibashi o Tataite Wataru* □ *Kusawake* □ *Onobori-san* □ *Sumeba Miyako* □ *Watari ni Fune*

Section Six: Idioms
More Cultural Keys   **83–101**

Asameshi Mae □ *Baka wa Shinanakya Naoranai* □ *Chan-Pon* □ *Deru Kui wa Utareru* □ *Hakoiri Musume* □ *Juubako no Sumi o [Yooji de] Tsutsuku* □ *Kataboo o Katsugu* □ *Kooin Ya no Gotoshi* □ *Koshikake* □ *Kusai Mono ni wa Futa o Suru* □ *Madogiwa Zoku* □ *Noren ni Udeoshi* □ *Onaji Kama no Meshi o Kutta* □ *Saji o Nageru* □ *Sashimi no Tsuma* □ *Sode no Shita* □ *Suna o Kamu Yoo* □ *Taikoban o Osu* □ *Yuushuu no Bi o Kazaru*

Indexes
Idioms listed by key images   **215**
Idioms listed alphabetically   **217**

101 Japanese Idioms

Understanding Japanese Language and
Culture Through Popular Phrases

Michael L. Maynard
Senko K. Maynard

Illustrations by Taki

Printed on recyclable paper

PASSPORT BOOKS
a division of *NTC Publishing Group*
Lincolnwood, Illinois USA

1995 Printing

Published by Passport Books, a division of NTC Publishing Group.
© 1993 by NTC Publishing Group, 4255 West Touhy Avenue,
Lincolnwood (Chicago), Illinois 60646-1975 U.S.A.
All rights reserved. No part of this book may be reproduced, stored
in a retrieval system, or transmitted in any form or by any means,
electronic, mechanical, photocopying, recording or otherwise, without
the prior permission of NTC Publishing Group.
Manufactured in the United States of America.

4 5 6 7 8 9 0 VP 9 8 7 6 5 4 3

Preface

The picturesque, idiomatic phrase captures the true essence of a society better than its equivalent prosaic description. Saying, for example, in Japanese, "it was packed like *sushi*," to describe the morning commuter train rush, is a more colorful, and, we think, preferable way of saying, "it was very crowded." Besides, "packed like *sushi*" (*sushizume*) comes directly from the culture; virtually every Japanese knows that *sushi* is packed tightly in boxes typically sold in take-out *sushi* shops and at train stations.

Thus the idiom resonates; it quickly establishes rapport. A mastery of Japanese idioms will help you understand the culture and speak a more authentic style of Japanese.

When you use idioms such as *sushizume* among your Japanese friends, colleagues, and business associates, you create emotional bonds that bring you closer to their culture. Since the Japanese are conditioned to believe that no people outside of the Japanese islands really know or care deeply about their culture, your use of a Japanese idiom in the appropriate context will both astound and delight them. More important, your command of Japanese idioms can lead to a deeper understanding of the Japanese people.

In this book, we introduce 101 popular Japanese idioms and expressions that we believe are both interesting and useful to students of Japanese language and culture. Each idiom is first introduced in Romanization, followed by Japanese orthography, and then a literal translation. Literal translations are deliberate, since combined with the visual, they lead you to the source of the phrase, which comes directly out of Japanese mythology, nature imagery, animal associations, or the human body as metaphor.

We have purposely translated *suzume no namida* as "tears of a sparrow," for example, because *suzume no namida* literally—and naturally—and in a Japanese way, says "small." Had we translated it loosely to mean "a tad," a great deal of the flavor and texture of the phrase would have been lost in the rendering.

Our literal translations of Japanese idioms are what set this book apart from other books on this same subject. In addition, background information on the origin or popular usage of each idiom offers valuable insights into Japanese culture.

We have also added a sample text to provide a context in which the idiom is generally used. To assist you in studying the language, sample text is presented in three stages: Romanization, Japanese orthography, and finally English. Translations and narratives are the authors' personal interpretations.

The book can be read from beginning to end in one sitting, or can be read in whatever order you choose. For handy reference, an alphabetical index of idioms as well as an index of idioms organized by key images are provided.

Extra study hint: After you've looked at each entry, go through the book a second time and place your hand over the top part of the left-hand page. See if you can recite the idiom in Japanese simply by looking at the illustration.

This book is intended for anyone who has an interest in learning more about the Japanese language and culture. Whether you are currently enrolled in a Japanese language course, are planning a trip to Japan, are curious about Japanese philosophy, or simply want to get to know your Japanese friends better, you will refer to this anthology of colorful Japanese idioms again and again.

Michael L. Maynard
Senko K. Maynard

Section One

Relating to Nature

Things That Grow   1–15

Water, Wind, and
Clouds   16–24

Gomasuri

ごますり

"sesame grinding"

(ingratiating oneself, apple-polishing, overtly flattering, toadying, sucking up to one's superiors)

When a person makes an overtly ingratiating remark, he or she is "grinding sesame seeds." Others call attention to the *gomasuri* either by saying the word, by (nonverbally) making motions with the fist over the palm of the other hand (simulating the grinding of roasted sesame seeds with a pestle and mortar), or by doing both. Like the messy sesame seeds ground up in the mortar, the person seeking favor is sticking to everything (one).

Sample text:
(Style: spoken/formal/male)

A: *Katoo-san iyoiyo kakarichoo ni shooshin rashii desu yo.*
B: *Yappari soo desu ka. Koko sannen kan zutto **gomasuri** o yatte kita n da kara, sorosoro kakarichoo ni naru daroo to wa omottemashita kedo ne.*

A: 加藤さんいよいよ係長に昇進らしいですよ。
B: やっぱりそうですか。ここ三年間ずっとごますりをやってきたんだから、そろそろ係長になるだろうとは思ってましたけどね。

A: I hear Mr. Kato is finally going to be promoted to section chief.
B: Just as I thought. I was thinking he would make section chief soon since he's been **apple-polishing** for the past three years.

Hana ni Arashi

花に嵐

"Blossoms bring storms."

(Life often brings misfortune at the time of great happiness.)

This fatalistic insight is a shortened version of *tsuki ni muragumo, hana ni arashi*, which is literally translated, "Clouds over the moon, storm over blossoms." It often seems that misfortune looms behind even the happiest moments.

Sample text
(Style: spoken/casual/female)

A: *Kekkon shite isshuukan de kyuuni goshujin ga nyuuin to wa okinodoku nee.*
B: *Shiawase ippai no tokoro ni zannen nee. Demo maa **"hana ni arashi"** to yuu kurai da kara, kooyuu koto mo unmei de shikata ga nai wa ne.*

A: 結婚して一週間で急に御主人が入院とはおきのどくねえ。
B: 幸せいっぱいのところに残念ねえ。でもまあ『花に嵐』と言うくらいだから、こういうことも運命で仕方がないわね。

A: It's too bad. Only married a week and her new husband got hospitalized.
B: Too bad, when she was so happy. But as they say, **"Life often brings misfortune at the time of great happiness."** It's simply fate. You can't help it.

3. Hana yori Dango

花よりだんご

"Sweets are preferred to flowers."

(The practical is preferred over the aesthetic.)

Every spring on the day of "flower viewing," Japanese traditionally travel to the countryside or visit parks to appreciate the beauty of nature. Yet human nature being what it is, people seem to show considerably more interest in the food than in the flowers.

Sample text:
(Style: spoken/casual/A=female, B=male)

A: *Iya da wa. Aki-chan tara sekkaku ohanami ni kita noni, tabete bakari ite.*

B: *Akio, omae wa yappari **hana yori dango** no taipu da na.*

A: いやだわ、あきちゃんたらせっかくお花見に来たのに、食べてばかりいて。

B: 昭男、お前はやっぱり花よりだんごのタイプだな。

A: Oh boy, Aki-chan is only interested in food, while we came to appreciate the cherry blossom trees in full bloom.

B: Akio, you're the type who **prefers the practical over the aesthetic**, aren't you?

Imo [no Ko] o Arau Yoo

芋〔の子〕を洗うよう

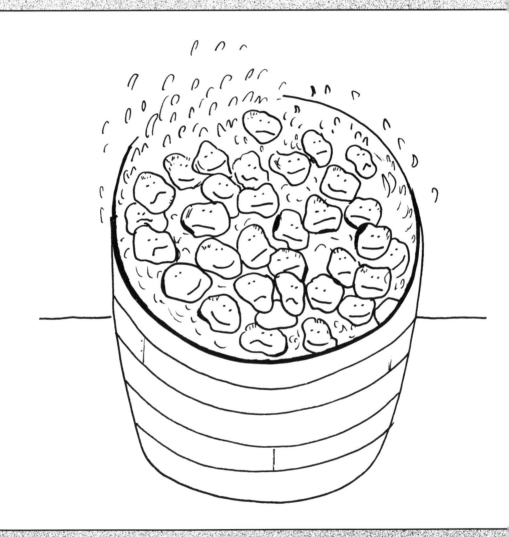

4. "like washing [a bucketful of] potatoes"

(so crowded you can hardly turn around, jam-packed, mobbed with people)

Summer weekends at the beach in Japan are impossible. The beaches are so crowded that you can hardly make space for your beach mat. When hordes of people play in the waist-deep ocean waters, wave after wave jostles them into each other. This commotion resembles a wooden bucketful of potatoes sloshing around while being washed by the agitator. Usage is restricted to water-related scenes.

Sample text:
(Style: written/informal)

Shichigatsu gejun no nichiyoobi, natsuyasumi ni haitta node, kodomozure no kazoku ga ooku, kaisui yokujoo wa **imo [no ko] o arau yoona** *konzatsuburi to natta.*

七月下旬の日曜日、夏休みに入ったので、子供連れの家族が多く、海水浴場は芋〔の子〕を洗うような混雑ぶりとなった。

Since it was a Sunday toward the end of July and summer vacation, there were a lot of families with kids, and the beach was **jam-packed**.

Iwanu ga Hana

言わぬが花

"Not saying is the flower."

(Some things are better left unsaid; silence is golden.)

Since one can never really "take back" what one says, there is a high premium on thinking things through before opening one's mouth. Much harm and nonsense can result from ill-chosen words. Thus the philosophical observation that "Not saying is the flower."

Sample text:
(Style: spoken/casual/female)

A: *Kare ni wa yappari himitsu ni shite okoo to omou no.*
B: *Soo ne.* ***"Iwanu ga hana"*** *tte kotowaza mo arushi ne.*

A: 彼にはやっぱり秘密にしておこうと思うの。
B: そうね。『言わぬが花』ってことわざもあるしね。

A: I think I'll keep it a secret from him.
B: That's good. You know the proverb, ***"Silence is golden."***

Korogaru Ishi ni Koke Musazu

転がる石に苔むさず

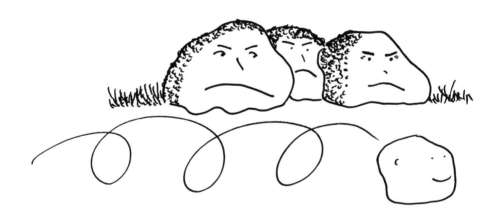

6.

"A stone that rolls gathers no moss."

(Perseverance pays off; patience is a virtue.)

For the Japanese, moss is something to be admired. Associated with beauty, moss grows on rocks and in pathways of old temples in places like Kyoto. Yet the stone that continues to tumble will never have moss. So this expression is often used to admonish others to stay put, to continue on in the same job. Ironically, this expression is also used by some Japanese to mean the very opposite, i.e., the meaning understood by Americans: keep moving or you'll get old.

Sample text:
(Style: written/informal)

*Ichido nyuusha shitara, shooshoo taihenna koto ga atte mo, zutto sono kaisha ni tsutometa hoo ga ii. **"Korogaru ishi ni koke musazu"** to iwareru yooni shokuba o amari kawaru no wa konomashii koto dewa nai.*

一度入社したら、少々大変なことがあっても、ずっとその会社に勤めたほうがいい。『転がる石に苔むさず』と言われるように職場を余り変わるのは好ましいことではない。

Once a person is employed, he or she is better off staying in the same company even when facing hardships. As the proverb ***"A stone that rolls gathers no moss"*** goes, it is not advisable to job-hop.

Minoru hodo
Atama no Sagaru
Inaho Kana

実る程頭の下がる稲穂かな

7. "The mature rice plant lowers its head."

(Maturity brings humility and respect for others.)

When rice is mature and ready to harvest, the heaviness at the top of the plant pulls it down low to the ground. Japanese see this as analogous to how the wisdom of years fills a man with humility and causes his head to bow heavily in his deep respect for life and nature.

Sample text:
(Style: spoken/casual A = female, B = male)

A: *Kondo irashita Tayama fukushachoo ne, rippana kata rashii wa nee. Mooshibun nai hitogara tte uwasa yo.*
B: *Soo na n da. Sore ni tottemo kenkyode, ibatteiru tokoro ga mattaku nai hito rashii ne.*
A: ***"Minoru hodo atama no sagaru inaho kana"*** *tte kotowaza ga pittari no kata yo.*

A: 今度いらした田山副社長ね、立派な方らしいわねえ。申し分ない人柄ってうわさよ。
B: そうなんだ。それにとっても謙虚で、いばっているところが全くない人らしいね。
A: 『実る程頭の下がる稲穂かな』ってことわざがピッタリの方よ。

A: You know the new vice-president Tayama. I hear he's a wonderful person. They say his personality is just ideal.
B: I agree. Besides, he seems to be humble and never arrogant.
A: He's the type that perfectly fits the proverb, ***"The mature rice plant lowers its head."***

Nemawashi

根回し

8. "preparing the roots for transplanting"

(informally securing prior approval, checking with everyone who counts before formal presentation, covering all the bases)

Nemawashi now is used worldwide to characterize the consensus-building nature of Japanese business practices. Literally, *nemawashi* means cutting off excess roots and wrapping the remaining roots with a straw mat for protection when transplanting the tree. In business terms it means an informal solicitation of agreement before formal submission of approval at a meeting.

Sample text:
(Style: spoken/casual/male)

A: *Kyoo no kaigi umaku iku ka naa.*
B: *Daijoobu daroo. Kanari **nemawashi** ni jikan o kakete kitashi, konkai no purojekuto wa buchoo mo noriki da kara.*

A: 今日の会議うまくいくかなあ。
B: 大丈夫だろう。かなり**根回し**に時間をかけてきたし、今回のプロジェクトは部長も乗り気だから。

A: I wonder if today's meeting is going to go well.
B: I think it will be fine. I spent a lot of time **covering all the bases**, and I know the manager likes our proposal.

Ne mo
Ha mo Nai

根も葉もない

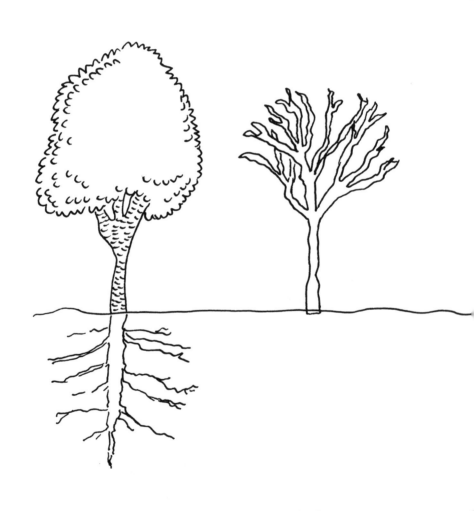

"without roots or leaves"

(groundless, unsubstantiated)

Roots give support to a tree much as facts give support to claims and allegations. Leaves validate the health of a tree, proving its life and vitality. With neither support (roots) nor evidence (leaves), the (tree) allegation cannot stand.

Sample text:
(Style: spoken/casual/A = male, B = female)

A: *Yamada-san no okusan, uwaki shiteru rashii yo.*
B: *Sonna koto, uso yo. Mattaku **ne mo ha mo nai** uwasa ni kimatteru wa.*

A: 山田さんの奥さん、浮気してるらしいよ。
B: そんなこと、うそよ。全く**根も葉も**ないうわさに決まってるわ。

A: Mrs. Yamada seems to be having an affair.
B: That's not true. That's a **groundless** rumor, for sure.

Sakura
さくら

"cherry blossom"

(a shill, a plant, a confederate)

This expression originates from the Edo period. A paid audience hired to applaud and cheer the show was seated in the section of the theater called "sakura."

Sample text:
(Style: spoken/casual/A = female, B = male)

A: *Nani ga sonnani okashii no kashira. Ano hito sakki kara zutto waratteru wa.*
B: **Sakura** *janai ka. Okashikumo nai mandan ni hitori de geragera waratteru n da kara.*

A: 何がそんなにおかしいのかしら。あの人さっきからずっと笑ってるわ。
B: さくらじゃないか。おかしくもない漫談にひとりでゲラゲラ笑ってるんだから。

A: What's so funny? That guy's been laughing awfully long.
B: Isn't he a **shill?** He's the only one laughing at the boring monologue.

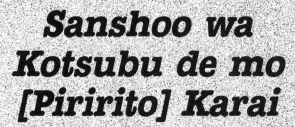

Sanshoo wa Kotsubu de mo [Piririto] Karai

山椒は小粒でも〔ぴりりと〕辛い

11. "Japanese peppers are hot, though small."

(small but powerful, a mighty mite, a person of ability although small in size)

Despite the small size of the Japanese pepper, it packs a powerful, spicy punch. The phrase suggests that size isn't the only determinant of strength or ability.

Sample text:
(Style: spoken/casual/male)

A: *Yaru naa. Kachoo mata shooshin da tte. Iyoiyo buchoo rashii.*
B: ***"Sanshoo wa kotsubu de mo karai"*** *tte ne.*

A: やるなあ、課長また昇進だって。いよいよ部長らしい。
B: 『山椒は小粒でも辛い』ってね。

A: Great! Our section chief has been promoted again. Looks like he's going to be a manager now.
B: Well, they say, ***"Japanese peppers are hot, though small."***

Takane no Hana

高嶺の花

"flower on a high peak"

(unrealizable desire, an unobtainable object, something out of one's reach)

Wistfully, a prize you can see but simply cannot reach. The beautiful flower is so far away that there is no real hope of picking it. Used to describe the object of desire which is completely out of reach.

Sample text:
(Style: spoken/casual/A=female, B=male)

A: *Yamamoto-kun ne, Yooko-san ni kataomoi na n da tte.*
B: *Sorya, minoranu koi da. Aite ga Yooko-san ja, **takane no hana** da kara naa.*

A：山本君ね、洋子さんに片思いなんだって。
B：そりゃ、実らぬ恋だ。相手が洋子さんじゃ、**高嶺の花**だからなあ。

A: You know Yamamoto, right? The rumor is he's in love with Yoko, but it's a one-way affair.
B: Oh boy! That kind of love is fruitless. His heart may be set on Yoko, but she really is **an unobtainable prize.**

Take o Watta Yoo

竹を割ったよう

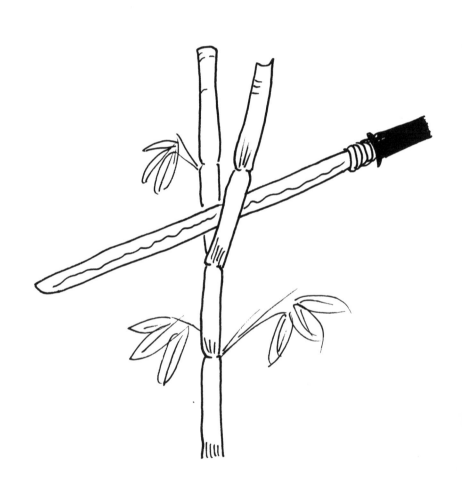

13. "as clean as a split bamboo"

(honest, frank, decisive, a straight-shooter)

When a bamboo pole is split lengthwise, the cut is true and straight—a clean split. *Take o watta yoo* describes a frank, decisive, and morally righteous person—usually in reference to a man, but sometimes in reference to a woman.

Sample text:
(Style: written/informal)

Nihonjin ga konomu dansei no imeeji wa, **take o watta yoona** *seikaku de, hakkiri shiteite ketsudanryoku no aru hito dearu koto ga ooi. Shikashi, ippan ni josei ni wa* **take o watta yoona** *seikaku to yuu yori, mushiro yasashisa ga nozomareru.*

日本人が好む男性のイメージは、竹を割ったような性格で、はっきりしていて決断力のある人であることが多い。しかし、一般に女性には竹を割ったような性格というより、むしろやさしさが望まれる。

The male image that the Japanese prefer is generally of a man who is **honest, frank, and decisive**. In a woman, however, they generally value tenderness much more highly than **frankness** or **decisiveness**.

Uri Futatsu

瓜二つ

14. "two halves of a cucumber"

(two peas in a pod, Tweedledum and Tweedledee, frick and frack)

Nature provides ample evidence of perfect symmetry. Split lengthwise, the two halves of a fruit or vegetable are perfectly identical. When two people are so much alike in appearance, they are *uri futatsu*.

Sample text:
(Style: spoken/casual/male)

A: *Ano kyoodai wa futatsu chigai da kedo, mattaku **uri futatsu** da nee. Kono aida, machigaechatte ne. Komatta yo, hontoni!*

A: あの兄弟は二つちがいだけど、全く瓜二つだねえ。この間、まちがえちゃってね。困ったよ、ほんとに!

A: Those brothers are two years apart, yet they're as alike as **two peas in a pod**. The other day I mistook one for the other, and was I embarrassed!

Yoraba Taiju no Kage

寄らば大樹の陰

15. "[Seek shelter in] the shade of a big tree."

(Choose secure and solid protection.)

Shade is figurative for protection. The tree you choose should be important and highly placed within your organization or in society in general. This expression is close in nuance to "it never hurts to have friends in high places."

Sample text:
(Style: written/informal)

Saikin no gakusei wa gakusha no kenkyuu teema dewa naku, gakusha no chimeido ya seijiryoku ni yotte kyooju o erabu keikoo ga aru. "Yoraba taiju no kage" to yuu wake ka.

最近の学生は学者の研究テーマではなく、学者の知名度や政治力によって教授を選ぶ傾向がある。『寄らば大樹の陰』というわけか。

There is a tendency among current students to choose an academic mentor not because of the professor's research interests but because of the professor's fame or political clout. I suppose it's because they say, ***"Seek shelter in the shade of a big tree."***

16. Ame ga Furoo to Yari ga Furoo to

雨が降ろうと槍が降ろうと

16. "even if rain falls or spears fall"

(no matter what, under any circumstances)

This expression reflects the firm determination Japanese are expected to have toward achieving their goal. Once the objective is set, after extensive deliberation and consideration, "come hell or high water," the project will be brought to a successful conclusion.

Sample text:
(Style: written/informal)

*Sankagetsu mo mae kara yotei shiteita ryokoo da kara, ashita wa **ame ga furoo to yari ga furoo to** shuppatsu suru tsumori da.*

三か月も前から予定していた旅行だから、明日は雨が降ろうと槍が降ろうと出発するつもりだ。

I've been planning this trip for three months, so I intend to leave tomorrow, **no matter what.**

Ame Futte Ji Katamaru

雨降って地固まる

"Rain firms the ground."

(Adversity builds character; the more challenges successfully met, the stronger one or a relationship becomes.)

Ame futte ji katamaru is often said to the bride and groom on their wedding day. In addition to meaning that bad experiences may actually be good, the expression admonishes young newlyweds that, for better or for worse, the ties that bind are strengthened through tough times.

Sample text:
(Style: spoken/formal)

A: *Kekkon seikatsu wa mochiron barairo no koto bakari dewa nai deshoo. **Ame futte ji katamaru** to iwaremasu yooni jinsei no kuroo o wakeatte suenagaku oshiawase ni.*

A: 結婚生活はもちろんバラ色のことばかりではないでしょう。雨降って地固まると言われますように人生の苦労を分け合って末長くお幸せに。

A: Married life will not always be rosy. But as the saying ***"Rain firms the ground"*** goes, I hope you will enjoy a happy and long relationship as you share the hardships of life.

Kaze no Tayori

風の便り

18. "message carried on the wind"

(a rumor, a story without source)

A letter delivered from the God of the Wind. Used to suggest news from an unnamed or an easily forgotten source. No direct line of communication exists. This expression compares with "a little birdie told me."

Sample text:
(Style: spoken/casual/A = male, B = female)

A: *Kyonen Amerika e kaetta Sumisu-san, ima doo shiteru ka naa.*
B: ***Kaze no tayori*** *de wa daigaku ni modotte benkyoo shiteiru rashii wa yo. Doko no daigaku ka shiranai kedo.*

A: 去年アメリカへ帰ったスミスさん、今どうしてるかなあ。
B: 風の便りでは、大学にもどって勉強しているらしいわよ。どこの大学か知らないけど。

A: You know that guy Smith, who went back to the U.S. last year? I wonder what he's up to nowadays.
B: I heard **a rumor** that he went back to school. I don't know which university, though.

Kumo o Tsukamu Yoo

雲をつかむよう

19. "like grasping a cloud"

(wishful thinking, impossible dream)

Since nobody can actually grasp a cloud, the expression denotes impossibility. From afar, a cloud has shape and form. Close-up, its gossamer essence dissipates at the touch. So when a not-so-talented sixteen-year-old declares that she's going to become a movie star, you can respond by saying it's a *kumo o tsukamu yoona* dream—a mild warning that the ambition or goal is highly unlikely to be realized.

Sample text:
(Style: spoken/casual/A = son, B = mother)

A: *Sakkyokuka ni naroo ka na.*
B: *Sonna **kumo o tsukamu yoona** koto bakari kangaeteiru kara itsu made tatte mo hitoridachi dekinai n desu yo.*

A: 作曲家になろうかな。
B: そんな雲をつかむようなことばかり考えているからいつまでたってもひとりだちできないんですよ。

A: You know, maybe I'll become a composer.
B: (Scolding) All you ever think about is ***impossible dreams*** like that! No wonder you've never been able to become financially independent.

Mizu ni Nagasu

水に流す

"to set things adrift"

(to forgive and forget, to let bygones be bygones)

A river carries bad memories away. By setting adrift the pain of a romantic breakup or the betrayal by a once-trusted friend, you start things anew. Once into the river's flow, the thing-to-forget heads downstream, never to return.

Sample text:
(Style: spoken/formal/female)

A: *Desukara, sore wa moo wasuremashoo. Mukashi no koto wa **mizu ni nagashite,** mata yari naoshimashoo yo.*
B: *Soo ne. Sore ga ichiban ii wa ne.*

A: ですから、それはもう忘れましょう。昔のことは水に流して、またやり直しましょうよ。
B: そうね。それが一番いいわね。

A: So let's forget about those days. **Let bygones be bygones** and try it again.
B: Yes. That looks like the best idea.

Mizu no Awa

水の泡

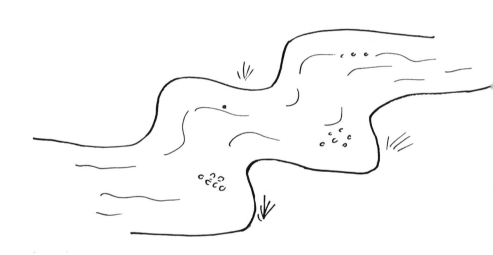

"bubbles on the water"

(all for nothing, effort in vain)

Stopping by a brook and observing water bubbles forming and disappearing, a Japanese may associate those bubbles with the transient nature of life. Used poetically to acknowledge that a great effort was in vain and now has vanished like bubbles on the water.

Sample text:
(Style: spoken/casual/A = female, B = male)

A: *Michio-kun no sakkaa ne, are dake doryokushite shiai ni sonaeta noni, toojitsu ame de chuushi ni natta n da tte.*
B: *Sankagetsu no doryoku mo **mizu no awa** ka. Kawaisooni na.*

A: 道男君のサッカーね、あれだけ努力して試合にそなえたのに、当日雨で中止になったんだって。
B: 三か月の努力も水の泡か。かわいそうにな。

A: This thing about Michio's soccer. He practiced so hard, but the game got cancelled because of rain.
B: Three months' ***effort was all in vain!*** Poor thing.

Mizu o Utta Yoo
水を打ったよう

22. "as if after scattered water"

(so quiet you could hear a pin drop, dead silence)

When performing the Tea Ceremony, it's customary to scatter water along the entrance path. This ritual indicates preparation. The water cleans; it moistens the soil to contain the dust. It also deadens the sound.

Sample text:
(Style: written/informal)

*Kontesuto no nyuushoosha no happyoo ga hajimatta. Shikaisha ga maiku no mae ni tatsu to, kaijoo wa isshun **mizu o utta yoona** shizukesa ni natta.*

コンテストの入賞者の発表がはじまった。司会者がマイクの前に立つと、会場は一瞬水を打ったような静けさになった。

The contest winners were about to be announced. When the Master of Ceremonies stepped up to the microphone, the crowd got **so quiet you could hear a pin drop.**

23.

Mizu Shoobai

水商売

"water business"

(entertainment business, a chancy trade)

Running water is not thought of as having a fixed rate of flow. Sometimes the water comes out strong, sometimes weak. Such is the "fluid" nature of the income levels for certain businesses. *Mizu shoobai* includes a variety of entertainment businesses—tea houses, entertainment spots, bars, massage parlors, and houses of prostitution. According to another etymological source, these businesses were situated along riverbanks, and thus the "water business."

Sample text:
(Style: spoken/casual/female)

A: *Mori-san no musukosan ne, kekkon shitai rashii kedo goryooshin ga hantai shiteru tte uwasa nee.*
B: *Soo na no yo. Nanishiro, aite ga **mizu shoobai** no de rashii no yo.*

A: 森さんの息子さんね、結婚したいらしいけどご両親が反対してるってうわさねえ。
B: そうなのよ。なにしろ、相手が水商売の出らしいのよ。

A: Mrs. Mori's son. It appears he wants to get married, but both parents are against it.
B: That's right. I hear that the bride-to-be is from the ***entertainment business.***

Yakeishi ni Mizu

焼け石に水

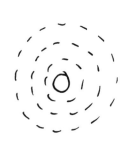

"water on a red-hot stone"

(a drop in the bucket, completely ineffective)

A drop of water thrown on a red-hot stone is of no consequence. Instead of cooling the stone, the drop of water evaporates in an instant. *Yakeishi ni mizu* expresses a grossly inadequate remedy to a problem.

Sample text:
(Style: spoken/casual/female)

A: *Kongetsu wa monosugoi akaji na no yo. Sukoshi shokuhi o setsuyaku shite mita kedo,* **yakeishi ni mizu** *de doonimo naranai wa.*

A: 今月はものすごい赤字なのよ。少し食費を節約してみたけど、焼け石に水でどうにもならないわ。

A: We are 'way in the red this month. I tried to spend less for groceries, but it's **a drop in the bucket.** I just don't know what to do.

Section Two

Creatures Large and Small

Birds and Beasts   25–36

Fish, Frogs, and
Others   37–46

Ashimoto kara Tori ga Tatsu

足もとから鳥が立つ

25. "Birds fly up from under one's feet."

(an unexpected departure, a surprise, a sudden happening)

What could be more startling than a pheasant or other ground-nesting bird flying up suddenly from in front of you? That's the feeling Japanese experience when a friend or an acquaintance leaves without warning. To be caught unawares.

Sample text:
(Style: spoken/casual/female)

A: *Tonari no manshon ni sundeita Kawakami-san, hikkoshita no?*
B: *Ee. Kyuuni Shidonii ni tenkin de ne. Mattaku* **"ashimoto kara tori ga tatsu"** *to wa, ano koto ne. Aru hi kyuuni satto hikiharatchatta no yo.*

A: となりのマンションに住んでいた川上さん、引っ越したの?
B: ええ。急にシドニーに転勤でね。全く『足もとから鳥が立つ』とは。あのことね。ある日急にサッとひき払っちゃったのよ。

A: Did Kawakami move, the guy next door in your condominium?
B: Yeah. He was unexpectedly transferred to Sydney. ***Such a surprise,*** you know. Suddenly one day he simply moved out.

53

Hane o Nobasu

羽根を伸ばす

"to stretch one's wings"

(to cut loose, to get rid of inhibition)

Away from home or the office, without constraints of position in society or conformity of rank within the Japanese company, one is more free to be adventurous. *Hane o nobasu* carries connotations of ''sowing a few wild oats'' as well as ''letting one's hair down.''

Sample text:
(Style: written/informal)

*Nihonjin wa shigoto nado de isogashii no ga suki da keredo, toki ni wa shigoto ya katei o hanarete, ryokoo ya rejaa o tanoshinde, **hane o nobasu** koto mo aru.*

日本人は仕事などで忙しいのが好きだけれど、時には仕事や家庭をはなれて、旅行やレジャーを楽しんで、羽根を伸ばすこともある。

Japanese prefer to be busy at work; but sometimes when they set foot outside the worksite and away from their homes to travel or pursue leisure activities, they really **cut loose.**

Karite Kita Neko no Yoo

借りてきた猫のよう

"like a borrowed cat"

(as shy and quiet as a kitten)

If a cat has a distant and aloof personality even within its own home, imagine how remote it would act in a strange place. The expression describes a shy, timid person who is not at home in his surroundings.

Sample text:
(Style: spoken/casual/female)

A: *Asobi ni kiteiru Takahashi-san no tokoro no Masao-kun, tottemo otonashii n da tte?*

B: *Soo rashii wa ne. Uchi de wa genki sugite komatteru rashii kedo, yoso no uchi de wa **karite kita neko no yooni** otonashii n datte.*

A: 遊びにきてる高橋さんのところの正夫君、とってもおとなしいんだって？

B: そうらしいわね。うちでは元気すぎて困ってるらしいけど、よそのうちでは借りてきた猫のようにおとなしいんだって。

A: I hear the Takahashi's boy Masao is visiting, but he's really quiet.

B: That's what I hear. He's almost hyperactive and troublesome at home, but in someone else's home, he's **as shy and quiet as a borrowed cat.**

Neko mo Shakushi mo

猫も杓子も

28. "even cats and rice ladles"

(everybody and his/her mother [brother])

According to one folk etymology, the rice ladle symbolizes housewives; since cats and housewives are virtually universal to Japanese households, the expression means "everybody." An opposite interpretation holds cats to be rare and rice ladles to be universal, so that the expression is all-inclusive of both rare and abundant items.

Sample text:
(Style: spoken/casual/female)

A: *Saikin mata sukaato take ga sukoshi mijikaku natta yoo ne.*
B: *Soo na no yo. Korede mata, **neko mo shakushi mo** mijikai sukaato ni naru n desho. Kosei ga nakute iya ni naru wa ne, mattaku.*

A: 最近またスカート丈が少し短くなったようね。
B: そうなのよ。これで又、**猫も杓子も**短いスカートになるんでしょ。個性がなくていやになるわね、全く。

A: It seems skirt lengths have shortened recently.
B: You noticed, too? Now **everybody and her mother** will be wearing shorter skirts. There's absolutely no individual style—I hate it!

Neko ni Koban

猫に小判

"a gold coin before a cat"

(pearls before swine)

Koban is a small oval-shaped gold coin which circulated in Japan prior to the Meiji Restoration of 1868. The expression is used when suggesting that not everyone can appreciate an object to the same degree. Similar to "do not cast pearls before swine," it means "don't offer anything of value and merit to those who are incapable of appreciating it."

Sample text:
(Style: spoken/casual/female)

A: *Sasaki-san no tokoro ne, musukosan no tame ni gurando piano o katta n da tte. Demo musukosan wa ongaku ni wa mattaku kyoomi ga nai mitai yo. **Neko ni koban** to wa ano koto ne.*

A: 佐々木さんのところね、息子さんのためにグランドピアノを買ったんだって。でも、息子さんは音楽には全く興味がないみたいよ。猫に小判とはあのことね。

A: I hear that Sasaki bought a grand piano for his son, but the son isn't interested in music at all. That is truly a case of ***"pearls before swine,"*** isn't it?

30.

Neko no Hitai

猫のひたい

"cat's forehead"

(extremely small in size)

Cats are not known to have high foreheads. The expression exaggerates the inadequacy of a space. *Neko no hitai* is often heard when prospective home buyers in Japan first see the size of their yard.

Sample text:
(Style: spoken/casual/A = female, B = male)

A: *Atarashii niwatsuki no uchi ni utsutta n desu tte?*
B: *Iya ne, niwa to ieru ka doo ka, honno* **neko no hitai** *no yoona uraniwa ga tsuiteru teido na n da.*

A: 新しい庭つきの家に移ったんですって?
B: いやね、庭と言えるかどうか、ほんの猫のひたいのような 裏庭がついてる程度なんだ。

A: I hear you moved into a single family home with a yard.
B: Yeah, but I'm not sure you can call it a yard; it's an ***extremely small*** backyard area.

Neko no Te mo Karitai

猫の手も借りたい

"willing to accept even the helping hand of a cat"

(swamped, shorthanded, "up to one's eyeballs" in work)

This phrase indicates an intense degree of need. Cats are useless when it comes to assisting people. If one will go so far as to accept even the help of a cat, one really is in desperate need.

Sample text:
(Style: spoken/casual/female)

A: *Ano, chotto gomennasai. Koko no jimusho, kyoo, hikkoshi de, **neko no te mo karitai** yoona isogashisa na no. Atode denwa suru wa.*

A: あの、ちょっとごめんなさい。ここの事務所、今日、引っ越しで、猫の手も借りたいような忙しさなの。あとで電話するわ。

A: Uh, sorry. You know at our office we're in the middle of a move today and we're **swamped.** I'll call you later.

Onaji Ana no Mujina

同じ穴のむじな

32. "badgers from the same hole"

(co-conspirators, brothers in crime)

Japanese fairy tales characterize badgers as sometimes villainous and at other times comical cheaters who play tricks on people. This is based on the fact that badgers and raccoons steal harvested produce from farmers. The phrase suggests a gang/group of bad guys.

Sample text:
(Style: spoken/casual/male)

A: *Murata-san no fusei ga hakkaku shite, onaji ka no Sakai-san mo taihen rashii yo.*

B: *Iya, Sakai-san mo **onaji ana no mujina** janai ka. Murata-san hitori de anna fusei ga dekiru wake nai yo.*

A: 村田さんの不正が発覚して、同じ課の酒井さんも大変らしいよ。

B: いや、酒井さんも**同じ穴のむじな**じゃないか。村田さんひとりであんな不正ができるわけないよ。

A: Murata's illegal doings have been discovered and Sakai, who is in the same section, seems to be very concerned.

B: But isn't Sakai a ***co-conspirator?*** Murata couldn't have done all that single-handedly, you know.

33.

Suzume no Namida

雀の涙

"sparrow's tears"

(very small amount, a tad)

The implication of this expression is "not enough" —one wishes it were more. If sparrows could cry, their tears would be tiny. Sparrows are commonly found throughout Japan and often represent ordinary people in Japanese folktales.

Sample text:
(Style: spoken/casual/male)

A: *Kyuuryoo agatta n da tte?*
B: *Iya, honno sukoshi.*
A: *Sonna koto nai daroo.*
B: *Agatta koto wa agatta kedo sa, honno **suzume no namida** de nee.*

A: 給料上がったんだって？
B: いや、ほんの少し。
A: そんなことないだろう。
B: 上がったことは上がったけどさ、ほんの雀の涙でねえ。

A: I hear you got a pay raise. Is it true?
B: Well. . . just a little.
A: You expect me to believe that?
B: OK, I got a pay raise, but it's such a ***small amount.***

34.

Tatsu Tori Ato o Nigosazu

立つ鳥後を濁さず

"Birds leave the water undisturbed."

(Leave on a good note; create a good impression when leaving for good.)

This is what we should remind people who are about to go into a nature preserve. Used most frequently in reference to one's place of work. Just as birds leave the water undisturbed, we should leave our current place of work undisturbed; i.e., in the best condition for one's replacement.

Sample text:
(Style: spoken/casual/A = male, B = female)

A: *Iyoiyo kaisha o yamete Nyuu Yooku e iku n da tte ne.*
B: *Ee. Sorede ima tottemo isogashii no yo. Iroiro seiri shite okanakereba naranai koto ga takusan atte. Soreni **"tatsu tori ato o nigosazu"** da kara.*

A: いよいよ会社を辞めてニューヨークへ行くんだってね。
B: ええ。それで今とっても忙しいのよ。いろいろ整理しておかなければならないことがたくさんあって。それに『立つ鳥後を濁さず』だから。

A: I hear you're quitting the company and going to New York soon.
B: That's right. So I'm really busy now. There are so many things I need to organize and put away. Besides, as the saying goes, ***"Birds leave the water undisturbed."***

35.

Tsuru no Hitokoe

鶴の一声

"the cry of the crane"

(voice of authority, unchallengeable order)

According to Japanese folklore, cranes live for a thousand years. It seems that old, white-haired village leaders live nearly as long. As the respected authority, the "wise old bird" is able to mobilize the village. Thus, a powerful voice from the acknowledged leader (regardless of age) is *tsuru no hitokoe*.

Sample text:
(Style: spoken/casual/male)

A: *Kyoo no kaigi wa zuibun shussekiritsu ga ii nee.*
B: *Sasaki-san shitteru daro? Kanojo no **tsuru no hitokoe** de isogashii noni minna atsumatta n da yo.*

A: 今日の会議は随分出席率がいいねえ。
B: 佐々木さん知ってるだろ？彼女の鶴の一声で忙しいのにみんな集まったんだよ。

A: Attendance at today's meeting was terrific, wasn't it?
B: You know Ms. Sasaki, don't you? It's her **voice of authority** that got everyone to attend.

Uma no Hone

馬の骨

"the bones of a horse"

(an unknown person with no references, a person of unknown background)

Imagine the skeleton of a horse half-buried in the sand. Who knows who the horse was? What of the horse's master? Nobody knows. That's the feeling behind the expression when applied to a newcomer in the tight-knit Japanese society. *Uma no hone* carries a heavy negative connotation when referring to an outsider.

Sample text:
(Style: spoken/formal/female)

A: *Kekkon mae no musume ga doko no **uma no hone** da ka wakaranai yoona otoko to tsukiatte wa ikemasen yo.*

A: 結婚前の娘がどこの馬の骨だか分からないような男とつきあってはいけませんよ。

A: Before marriage a girl should not go out with **a man of unknown background.**

"little fish grinding their teeth"

(of no consequence, powerless)

If sharks were to grind their teeth, it might be a big deal. Shock waves would radiate in all directions. But a bunch of little fish furiously grinding their teeth is of no consequence. Who would know? Who would care?

Sample text:
(Style: spoken/casual/male)

A: *Konnendo no shinnyuu buin wa monku bakari itteru ne.*
B: *Ki ni shinai, ki ni shinai. Doose **gomame no hagishiri** na n da kara, ima made doori ni yatte ikeba ii sa.*

A: 今年度の新入部員は文句ばかり言ってるね。
B: 気にしない、気にしない。どうせごまめの**歯ぎしり**なんだから、今まで通りにやっていけばいいさ。

A: This year's new club members do nothing but complain.
B: Don't worry, don't worry. What they say is **of no consequence** anyway. We'll just carry on as we always have.

Hachi no Su o Tsutsuita Yoo

蜂の巣をつついたよう

"like poking a beehive"

(bedlam, chaotic, frenzied)

The impression is that of a swarm of noisy bees buzzing around in a frenzy of confusion. Complete bedlam that one is not happy about.

Sample text:
(Style: written/informal)

Nigakki no hajime. Sensei ga kuru mae, kodomo tachi wa natsuyasumi no hanashi ya shukudai no koto nado, waiwai gayagaya. Marude **hachi no su o tsutsuita yoona** *sawagashisa da.*

二学期のはじめ。先生が来る前、子供達は夏休みの話や宿題のことなど、ワイワイガヤガヤ。まるで蜂の巣をつついたような騒がしさだ。

The beginning of the second semester. Before the teacher shows up, the children are chatting about their summer vacations and about their assignments. It's **chaotic.**

Hippari Dako

ひっぱりダコ

"a spread-eagled octopus"

(Mr./Mrs./Ms. Popularity, a person in great demand, being pulled in all directions)

This expression originates from the way an octopus is stretched out to dry. All eight legs are spread out and stretched to their limits. Thus, when the pretty young starlet or the renowned architect is suddenly in great demand, the impression is like a *hippari dako*.

Sample text:
(Style: A=informal/male, B=formal/male)

A: *Ano shinjin kashu, saikin zuibun ninki ga dete kita ne.*

B: *Soo na n desu yo. Moo iroirona tokoro kara **hippari dako** de ne. Uchi no zasshi no intabyuu toru no mo taihenna kurai na n desu yo.*

A: あの新人歌手、最近ずいぶん人気が出てきたね。

B: そうなんですよ。もういろいろなところからひっぱりダコ でね。うちの雑誌のインタビューとるのも大変なくらいな んですよ。

A: That new singer is really getting popular.

B: She sure is! She's **in great demand;** actually it was difficult booking her for our magazine interview.

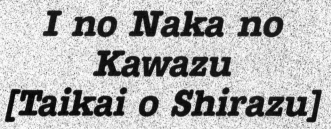

I no Naka no Kawazu [Taikai o Shirazu]

40.

井の中の蛙〔大海を知らず〕

40.

"A frog in the well [doesn't know the sea]."

(a provincial, one who has never seen the world)

Used to advocate greater travel beyond the Japanese islands, it captures the Japanese sense of awareness of being like a frog in a well. Comfortable as the well may be, it is but a small part of the whole world. Japanese teachers often recite this proverb to encourage their students to progress beyond the circumstances into which they were born.

Sample text:
(Style: written/informal)

*Ningen wa dare demo onaji basho ni nagaku sumu to, **i no naka no kawazu** ni naru. Dakara tokidoki jibun no sodatta kankyoo, jibun no sumi nareta sekai to chigau soto no ookina sekai ni mo, jibun jishin o oite miru koto ga taisetsu dearu.*

人間は誰でも同じ場所に長く住むと、井の中の蛙になる。だから時々自分の育った環境、自分の住み慣れた世界と違う外の大きな世界にも、自分自身を置いてみることが大切である。

When a person remains in the same location for many years, he or she becomes *a frog in the well.* So it is important sometimes to place ourselves in the wide world outside of the environment where we grew up or the narrow world we have grown accustomed to.

Ka no Naku Yoona Koe

蚊のなくような声

"a voice like the cry of a mosquito"

(a faint, almost inaudible voice)

Like a mosquito that buzzes in and out of your range, the person's voice is faint and hard to hear.

Sample text:
(Style: spoken/formal/female)

A: *Sonna **ka no naku yoona koe** de wa minna ni kikoemasen yo. Motto ookina koe de moo ichido itte minasai.*

A: そんな蚊のなくような声ではみんなに聞こえませんよ。もっと大きな声でもう一度言ってみなさい。

A: Nobody can hear your ***faint*** voice. Try saying it again, only louder.

Manaita no Ue no Koi

まな板の上の鯉

42. "carp on the cutting board"

(doomed, in the hands of God, at the mercy of fate)

This fatalistic expression is used when one feels helpless to control one's immediate destiny. The foreboding overtone comes from the knowledge of what inevitably befalls a fish laid out on a cutting board.

Sample text:
(Style: spoken/casual/A=female, B=male)

A: *Murata-san ne, shakkin ga kasanatte toosan sunzen na n da tte. Ato wa ginkoo no dekata shidai to yuu koto rashii wa.*

B: *Soreja marukkiri **manaita no ue no koi** janai ka. Shinseki ka shiriai no tsute de doonika naranai no ka ne.*

A: 村田さんね、借金がかさなって倒産寸前なんだって。あとは銀行の出方次第ということらしいわ。

B: それじゃまるっきりまな板の上の鯉じゃないか。親戚か知り合いのつてでどうにかならないのかね。

A: I hear that Mr. Murata is in great debt and is on the verge of bankruptcy. It all seems to depend on the bank now.

B: He's **doomed** then. Can't his relatives and friends do something about it?

Mushi no Iki

虫の息

43.

"the breath of an insect"

(near one's death, almost dead)

Since insects are small, imagine how faint their breath must be. The chances of recovery are extremely slim for a man whose breath is as faint as that of an insect.

Sample text:
(Style: spoken/formal/female)

A: *Tanaka-san no oniisan, mattaku kinodokuni nee.*
   Kootsuu jiko de nakunatta n desu tte ne.
B: *Ee, soo na n desu tte. Ookina jiko de ne, byooin ni*
   *tsuita toki wa moo **mushi no iki** datta rashii n desu yo.*

A: 田中さんのお兄さん、全く気の毒にねえ。交通事故で亡く
   なったんですってね。
B: ええ、そうなんですって。大きな事故でね、病院に着いた
   時はもう**虫の息**だったらしいんですよ。

A: Tanaka's brother, what a tragedy! I hear he was killed
   in a traffic accident.
B: Yes, that's what I heard, too. It was a pretty serious
   accident. It seems he was ***almost dead*** by the time he
   arrived at the hospital.

Nakitsura ni Hachi

泣き面に蜂

44

"The bee [stings] when you're already crying."

(When it rains, it pours; bad things come in threes.)

When someone has been hit simultaneously with several bad breaks, it may be consoling to hear a friend say, *"Nakitsura ni hachi."* The philosophical surety of the phrase reminds Japanese that misfortune may indeed come in twos (or even threes).

Sample text:
(Style: spoken/casual/male)

A: *Yukari wa kinoo sensei ni shikararete nakinagara kaette kuru tochuu, Masao-kun ni nagurareta rashii n da. Mattaku **nakitsura ni hachi** to wa kono koto da na.*

A: ゆかりはきのう先生にしかられて泣きながら帰ってくる途中、正夫君になぐられたらしいんだ。全く**泣き面に蜂**とはこのことだな。

A: Yesterday, apparently, Yukari's teacher scolded her, and then as she was crying on her way home, Masao beat her up. It's really true: ***"When it rains, it pours."***

Saba o Yomu

さばを読む

"to read the mackerel"

(to manipulate the figures to one's advantage, to offer false numbers intentionally, to inflate or deflate figures)

Among fish caught in nets, mackerel are so little valued that Japanese fishermen may not bother to count them. Often the rough estimates of mackerel have been highly inflated, giving rise to the use of the phrase "reading the mackerel" to indicate the practice of "guesstimating" in one's own favor.

Sample text:
(Style: spoken/casual/A = female, B = male)

A: *Kono kaikei, zuibun takai to omowanai? Nomimono yonjuuhachinin bun tte aru kedo.*
B: *Kanari **saba o yonderu** n janai ka. Kaisha barai da kara wakaranai to omotteiru n daroo.*

A: この会計、ずいぶん高いと思わない？ 飲みもの四十八人分ってあるけど。
B: かなりさばを読んでるんじゃないか。会社払いだからわからないと思っているんだろう。

A: Don't you think this bill is awfully high? They list 48 drinks!
B: They must be ***inflating the figures.*** They probably figure nobody will catch it since the company's paying for it.

46. Tade Kuu Mushi mo Sukizuki

たで食う虫も好き好き

46. # "Some bugs prefer bitters."

(There is no accounting for tastes; some prefer nettles.)

This Japanese proverb acknowledges the reality that people have different tastes. Also used to warn people not to judge others by one's own taste. *Tade* is smartweed, a bitter tasting plant. Yet some insects prefer it.

Sample text:
(Style: spoken/casual/A = male, B = female)

A: *Aitsu naze anna ii okusan to wakarete, mata henna onna to saikon shita n daroo.*
B: *Datte **"tade kuu mushi mo sukizuki"** tte yuu deshoo.*

A: あいつなぜあんないい奥さんと別れて、又変な女と再婚したんだろう。
B: だって、『たで食う虫も好き好き』って言うでしょう。

A: Why did he divorce such a good woman and remarry such a weirdo?
B: Oh well, you know, ***there's no accounting for tastes.***

Section Three

The Human Body

Abata mo Ekubo

あばたもえくぼ

47. "Pockmarks are [seen as] dimples."

(Love is blind.)

Abata mo ekubo is another way of saying, "Beauty is in the eye of the beholder." But in this Japanese expression, the beholder is almost always a man who is beholding a woman. Her face may not have physical beauty, but her personality makes her attractive to him.

Sample text:
(Style: spoken/casual/female)

A: *Akio-kun ne, kon'yaku shita n da tte.*
B: *Hee, doko no ojoosan to? Kireina hito?*
A: *Kirei to yuu wake demo nai kedo, kawaii ko yo. Soreni sukini nareba* **abata mo ekubo** *da kara ne.*

A: 昭男君ね、婚約したんだって。
B: へえ、どこのお嬢さんと？　きれいな人？
A: きれいと言うわけでもないけど、かわいい子よ。それに好きになればあばたもえくぼだからね。

A: You know Akio—I hear he got engaged.
B: Really? With whom? Is she pretty?
A: I wouldn't call her pretty, but she's cute. Besides, you know **love is blind.**

Agura o Kaku

あぐらをかく

"to sit crosslegged"

(to rest on one's laurels, to coast, to be complacent)

Sitting on the edge of one's chair with both feet firmly planted on the ground shows eagerness, enthusiasm, and a spirit of trying hard to succeed. In contrast, a relaxed pose of sitting on a cushion with one's legs crossed means to coast, to rest on one's laurels.

Sample text:
(Style: spoken/casual/male)

A: *Doose moo tairitsu suru aite wa inai daroo to omotte, itsumade mo shachoo no za ni **agura o kaite** irareru to omottara oomachigai da.*

A: どうせもう対立する相手はいないだろうと思って、いつまでも社長の座にあぐらをかいていられると思ったら大間違いだ。

A: You think you have no competitors; but it's a mistake to believe that you can sit forever in the company's president's position and ***rest on your laurels.***

Ashimoto o Miru

足もとを見る

"to look at someone's feet"

(to exploit someone's weakness in negotiation, to charge what the traffic will bear)

According to Japanese etymological sources, *ashimoto o miru* comes from the Feudal Age when the palanquin carriers would examine the legs and feet of prospective customers to judge their level of exhaustion, then raise the fare accordingly.

Sample text:
(Style: spoken/casual/male)

A: *Kinoo wa taihen datta yo. Nakagawa to niji made nonjatte sa. Kaeri no takushii ne, **ashimoto o mirarechatte,** takushiidai, zuibun torareta n da.*

A: きのうは大変だったよ。中川と二時まで飲んじゃってさ。帰りのタクシーね、**足もとを見られちゃって**、タクシー代、随分とられたんだ。

A: Last night was a disaster. I ended up drinking with Nakagawa until two in the morning. And of course, the taxi driver **took advantage of my condition** and overcharged me like crazy.

50. *Ashi o Arau*

足を洗う

"to wash one's feet"

(to start over [after discarding a bad situation], to go straight)

Menial, less prestigious jobs often require working outdoors and sometimes even working barefooted. So to wash one's feet figuratively means to give up a lowly job or to rise up from a morally wrong way of life (crime).

Sample text:
(Style: written/informal)

*Ichido furyoo nakama ni haittara, nakanaka nuke dasenai mono da. Yakuza no sekai to onaji de, aru shuudan ni nakamairi shite shimau to ningen wa kantanni wa **ashi o araenai** mono dearu.*

一度不良仲間に入ったら、なかなか抜け出せないものだ。やくざの世界と同じで、ある集団に仲間入りしてしまうと人間は簡単には足を洗えないものである。

When a man becomes a member of a gang, it's very difficult to break away from it. As in the case of the world of *yakuza* [Japanese organized crime], once you're a part of it, it is not an easy thing **to go straight.**

51.

Atama ga Sagaru

頭が下がる

"One's head is bowed."

(to take off one's hat to another, to acknowledge the exceptional effort of others)

When moved by another's extraordinary effort, one's head, voluntarily or involuntarily lowers in respect. Such is the reaction depicted by *atama ga sagaru*.

Sample text:
(Style: spoken/casual/female)

A: *Hontooni ano hito no doryoku o miru to,* **atama ga sagaru** *omoi ga suru wa.*
B: *Dare no koto?*
A: *Hora, itsumo toshokan de benkyoo shiteiru wakai hito, Maeda-san tte yuu n janakatta?*

A: 本当にあの人の努力を見ると、頭が下がる思いがするわ。
B: 誰のこと？
A: ほら、いつも図書館で勉強している若い人、前田さんって言うんじゃなかった？

A: Watching that guy work, I really have **to take off my hat to him!**
B: What guy?
A: You know, that young guy who's always studying in the library. Wasn't his name Maeda?

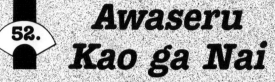

52.
Awaseru
Kao ga Nai
合わせる顔がない

52. "having no face to face someone"

(to be ashamed, not knowing how to face someone)

This idiom captures the deep concern Japanese have for maintaining face. "Face," of course, means one's positive image, one's public identity and correct behavior within the community. The "having no face" part of the expression can be interpreted as "not knowing what expression to wear," or "not knowing even how to compose one's expression" when having to face someone at a time when one feels deeply ashamed.

Sample text:
(Style: spoken/formal)

A: *Sumimasen. Konkai no purojekuto ga umaku ikanakatta no wa zenbu watashi no fuchuui ni yoru mono desu. Mattaku **awaseru kao ga arimasen**.*

A: すみません。今回のプロジェクトがうまくいかなかったのは全部私の不注意によるものです。全く**合わせる顔があり**ません。

A: I'm sorry. It was due to my carelessness that the project didn't go well. ***I have no idea how to face you*** . . . .

Haragei

腹芸

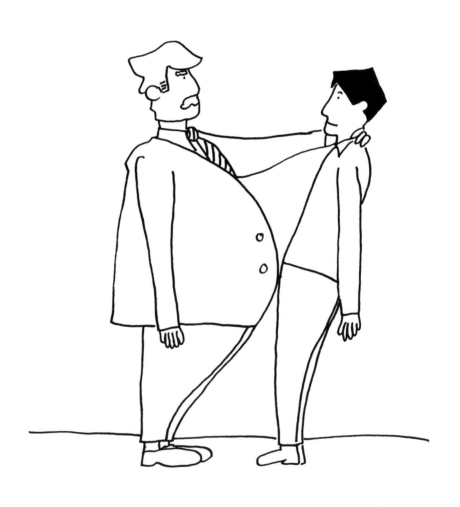

"belly performance"

(intuitive decision making, going on a gut feeling, negotiating without the use of direct words)

The origin of the word *haragei* is a drama performed on the belly of a person lying down, or a skit performed with a face painted on one's belly. From this comes the meaning of a theatrical strategy to communicate to others without words. Today *haragei* is thought of as a nonverbal, intuitive problem-solving technique requiring experience, sensitivity, and a keen knowledge of others.

Sample text:
(Style: spoken/casual/male)

A: *Kondo no chiji wa oomono da nee. Hito o ugokasu sokojikara ga aru yoo da.*
B: *Soo rashii. Nanishiro **haragei** ni taketa hito da tte yuu uwasa ga aru kurai da kara.*

A: 今度の知事は大物だねえ。人を動かす底力があるようだ。
B: そうらしい。何しろ腹芸にたけた人だっていううわさがあるくらいだから。

A: Our new governor is a real ''Mover and Shaker.'' He seems to have a knack for mobilizing people into action.
B: That's what I hear, too. People say it's because his **intuitive negotiating technique** is very effective.

Ishin Denshin

以心伝心

"reading each other's heart"

(reading each other's heart or mind; wordless, yet deep understanding between two [close] people)

Wordless yet total communication between two people, as if one heart is in direct contact with the other. Couples who have been married for 50 years may have *ishin denshin*. Co-workers, business associates, and friends are also capable of this harmonious relationship.

Sample text:
(Style: spoken/casual/A = female, B = male)

A: *Keiyakusho o kawashite konakatta no?*
B: *Ii n da yo. Soo nanimo kamo bunsho ni shinakute mo. Aitsu to ore to wa, nagai aida no tsukiai de **ishin denshin** da kara ne.*

A: 契約書を交わしてこなかったの？
B: いいんだよ。そう何もかも文書にしなくても。あいつとおれとは、長い間のつきあいで**以心伝心**だからね。

A: Didn't you two sign a contract?
B: It's OK. We don't need to put everything down in words. He and I have been friends for a long time; we **read each other's mind.**

Kao ga Hiroi

顔が広い

"wide-faced"

(to be widely known, to have a large circle of acquaintances, to have many contacts)

To be established in business or to be respected in society, it is important to be *kao ga hiroi*. The *kao ga hiroi* person is often the community leader or the authority figure in the profession. He or she has many contacts in the community and is expected to perform a paternal or maternal role.

Sample text:
(Style: spoken/casual/A = female, B = male)

A: *Sachiko-san mata omiai na n desu tte.*
B: *Tsugi kara tsugi e to yoku miai banashi ga hairu nee.*
A: *Otoosan ga* **kao ga hiroi** *kara iroirona tokoro kara hanashi ga aru n deshoo.*

A: 幸子さんまたお見合いなんですって。
B: 次から次へとよく見合い話がはいるねえ。
A: お父さんが**顔が広い**からいろいろなところから話があるんでしょう。

A: Sachiko has another *omiai**, right?
B: She sure gets those *miai* requests one after another, doesn't she?
A: **Everybody knows her father,** so *omiai* requests must come in from everywhere.

**(O)miai* refers to an arranged meeting with a potential marriage partner.

Katami ga Semai

肩身がせまい

56.

"narrow shoulders"

(a feeling of inferiority or inadequacy)

When in the presence of others who are superior in some respect, one's feelings of inferiority may be intensified. The physical manifestation of this feeling is a shrinking into oneself. The Japanese picture this reaction as a drawing in of the shoulders.

Sample text:
(Style: spoken/casual/male)

A: *Ano paatii wa gakusha to chishikijin no atsumari de ne. Watashi no yooni gakureki no nai mono ni wa chotto **katami ga semai** yo.*

A: あのパーティーは学者と知識人の集まりでね。私のように学歴のない者にはちょっと肩身がせまいよ。

A: The people at that party were mostly scholars and intellectuals. A person like me, who doesn't have an educational background, **feels kind of inadequate.**

Koshi ga Hikui

腰が低い

"low-waisted"

(very polite, modest or humble)

It's probably fair to say that Japanese are preoccupied with hierarchies. Status is indicated physically by one's posture in relation to others. To bend a little, to lower one's head, or to bow a deep bow is to position oneself vis-à-vis a person of higher rank. Thus, *koshi ga hikui* is a compliment—especially to one who, by virtue of wealth or fame, has attained high status.

Sample text:
(Style: spoken/casual/male)

A: *Tanaka shachoo, daigaisha no shachoo da kedo chittomo ibaru koto ga nai n da na. **Koshi ga hikukute** sa. Dakara minna ni sukareru n daroo na.*

A: 田中社長、大会社の社長だけどちっともいばることがないんだな。腰が低くてさ。だからみんなに好かれるんだろうな。

A: President Tanaka. You know, even though he's the president of a big company, he never puts on airs. He's always **modest.** That's why he is liked by everyone.

Mimi ga Itai

耳が痛い

58.

"My ears hurt."

(an acknowledgment that someone's criticism of oneself is correct; an indication of a prick of conscience, as if saying "you found me out.")

Some say that, despite Japan's economic might, its people are pretty simple. To say "my ears hurt," when words of criticism are hurled one's way, is direct and disarming. It's a way of saying "you got me." Implicit in the phrase is the recognition of wrongdoing.

Sample text:
(Style: spoken/casual/male)

A: *Isogashii, isogashii tte iinagara, muda banashi bakari shiteiru kara shigoto ga zenzen susumanai n da yo.*
B: *Iyaa, sono toori. **Mimi ga itai** na.*

A: 忙しい、忙しいって言いながら、むだ話ばかりしているから仕事が全然進まないんだよ。
B: いやあ、その通り。耳が痛いな。

A: You say you're busy, but you waste your time chit-chatting. That's why you can't get your work done.
B: You're right. **You got me!**

Ryooyaku Kuchi ni Nigashi

良薬口に苦し

59. "Good medicine tastes bitter in the mouth."

(Good advice is often unpleasant and difficult to accept.)

Teaches that one cannot expect to hear only good news in life. Sometimes, although painful, it is good medicine to taste the bitter truth. It is implicit in the statement that the speaker "cares enough" to speak with unusual candor.

Sample text:
(Style: spoken/casual/male)

A: *Itsumo kachoo kara komakaku chuui sareru no ga tamaran yo.*
B: ***"Ryooyaku kuchi ni nigashi"*** *tte yuu janai ka. Ima wa nigai to omottemo atode yokatta to kitto omou yo.*

A: いつも課長から細かく注意されるのがたまらんよ。
B: 『良薬口に苦し』って言うじゃないか。今はにがいと思ってもあとで良かったときっと思うよ。

A: I can't stand being constantly corrected in detail by the manager.
B: You know, they say, ***"Good medicine tastes bitter in the mouth."*** You may think these detailed corrections are unpleasant now but later on you'll realize their benefit.

Shinzoo ga Tsuyoi

心臓が強い

60.

"strong-hearted"

(having nerve or gall, impervious to subtleties)

Shinzoo ga tsuyoi describes a socially bold, cheeky person. Usually considered a negative trait, the phrase also may refer to having the courage (or gall) to behave against what is normally expected, like an employee who questions his boss, or a student who challenges the teacher.

Sample text:
(Style: spoken/casual/A = female, B = male)

A: *Sachiko-san, daijoobu kashira. Minna o daihyoo shite fuhei o ii ni itta kedo.*
B: *Kanojo nara daijoobu sa. **Shinzoo ga tsuyoi** kara hakkiri monku ieru daro.*

A: 佐知子さん、大丈夫かしら。みんなを代表して不平を言いに行ったけど。
B: 彼女なら大丈夫さ。**心臓が強い**からはっきり文句言えるだろ。

A: I wonder if Sachiko is OK. She went to register a complaint on behalf of the group.
B: She'll be fine. She **has a lot of nerve;** she'll tell them exactly what they did wrong.

Shiroi Me de Miru

白い目で見る

61. "to look at someone with white eyes"

(to look coldly upon, to cast an unwelcoming glance)

This expression means to treat someone with disdain bordering on contempt. This is an especially appropriate phrase when the person is outside of one's group. Why *shiroi* (white) eyes? One theory is that eyes without pupils would have a cold, ghostly look analogous to a scornful rebuke.

Sample text:
(Style: spoken/casual/female)

A: *Kondo hikkoshite kita Inoue-san ne. Ano hito wa honto no okusan janakute, aijin na n datte. Sore ga shirete kara mawari no shufu wa minna **shiroi me de mihajimeta** yoo yo.*

A: 今度引っ越してきた井上さんね。あの人はほんとの奥さんじゃなくて、愛人なんだって。それが知れてからまわりの主婦はみんな白い目で見はじめたようよ。

A: You know the Inoues who just moved in? I hear Mrs. Inoue is not the wife, but a mistress. Once the news spread, housewives in the neighborhood **began to look at her coldly.**

62. *Tsura no Kawa ga Atsui*

面の皮が厚い

62. "The skin on one's face is thick."

(uncommonly rude, having too much nerve, inconsiderate by nature)

The ideal face in Japan figuratively has a thin layer of skin so as to respond with sensitivity to others. In contrast, a thick-skinned, un-Japanese face reflects an inability to blush (to show shame), to reveal vulnerability, or to show empathy.

Sample text:
(Style: spoken/casual/female)

A: *Murai-san ne, jibun ga wasureta noni, zenzen hansei shinai no yo. Sono kuse hoka no wasureta hito ni monku itteru no.*

B: *Sooyuu no wa **tsura no kawa ga atsui** tte yuu no yo. Futsuu no hito nara sonna koto zettai dekinai to omou wa.*

A: 村井さんね、自分が忘れたのに、ぜんぜん反省しないのよ。そのくせ他の忘れた人に文句言ってるの。

B: そういうのは**面の皮が厚い**って言うのよ。普通の人ならそんなこと絶対できないと思うわ。

A: You know Ms. Murai, she herself forgot, but she wouldn't think of apologizing! Instead, she criticizes everybody else who forgot.

B: That's what I call being **uncommonly rude.** A normal person could never do such a thing!

Ude o Migaku

腕をみがく

"to polish one's arms"

(to work at mastering one's craft, to improve and cultivate one's skill)

Ude o migaku is most often used in advice to the young, warning them constantly to improve their skills. In Japan discipline and training are considered essential to success in any field.

Sample text:
(Style: spoken/formal/male)

A: *Wakai uchi ni isshookenmei **ude o migaite** okanai to shoorai komarimasu yo.*
B: *Isshookenmei yatteru n desu kedo, nakanaka omou yooni dekinakute.*

A: 若いうちに一生懸命**腕**をみがいておかないと将来困りますよ。
B: 一生懸命やってるんですけど、なかなか思うようにできなくて。

A: You'll be in trouble later on if you don't **work at mastering your craft** while you are young.
B: I'm doing my best, but I don't seem to be able to achieve what I want.

64.
Ushirogami o Hikareru Omoi
後ろ髪を引かれる思い

64. "a feeling as if one's hair is being pulled back"

(a feeling of much reluctance, a feeling of leaving one's heart behind)

A deep feeling of guilt for discarding one option in life in favor of another. Japanese feel a lingering tug of loyalty toward the discarded option. The tug, however, is not at the heart strings but at the hairs at the back of the head.

Sample text:
(Style: written/informal)

*Ima kara sannen mae, toshioita fubo o nokoshite Tookyoo ni dete kita. Sono toki no **ushirogami o hikareru omoi** wa ima mo wasurerarenai.*

今から三年前、年老いた父母を残して東京に出てきた。その時の後ろ髪を引かれる思いは今も忘れられない。

Three years ago, I left my aged parents and moved to Tokyo. I still can't forget that strong **feeling of reluctance** I felt then.

65. Ushiroyubi o Sasareru Yoo

後ろ指をさされるよう

"like having a finger pointed at one's back"

(being the object of social contempt, scorn, and criticism)

Social control through shame is highly developed in Japan. Japanese are keenly sensitive to being the object of scorn or ostracism. This expression conveys the feeling that everyone is pointing an accusatory finger at one's back for one's shameful conduct.

Sample text:
(Style: spoken/casual/A = female, B = male)

A: *Hamada-san ne, kaisha ni uso itte katteni ryokoo shita n da tte. Watashi mo yatte miyoo ka na.*

B: *Iya, hito ni **ushiroyubi o sasareru yoona** koto wa shinai hoo ga ii yo. Kitto ato de kookai suru kara.*

A: 浜田さんね、会社にうそ言って勝手に旅行したんだって。私もやってみようかな。

B: いや、人に後ろ指をさされるようなことはしない方がいいよ。きっとあとで後悔するから。

A: You know Ms. Hamada. She lied to the company and went off on a vacation. I'm thinking about doing something like that myself.

B: You really shouldn't do something you'll **be socially criticized for.** You'll regret it later, I'm sure.

Section Four

From One to Ten and More

Chiri mo Tsumoreba Yama to Naru

66.

ちりも積もれば山となる

66.

"piled-up specks of dust become a mountain."

(Little things add up; "Mountains are made from grains of sand." Small efforts, when accumulated, bring great success.)

This expression teaches the moral that, little by little and bit by bit, one's persistent efforts will lead to achievement. Even the smallest of efforts, however trivial they may seem at the time, will contribute toward one's ultimate success.

Sample text:
(Style: spoken/casual/A = male, B = female)

A: *Okane sonna sukoshi zutsu no chokin ja, nakanaka tamaranai ne.*
B: *Demo **"chiri mo tsumoreba yama to naru"** tte yuu desho.*

A: お金そんな少しずつの貯金じゃ、なかなかたまらないね。
B: でも、『ちりも積もれば山となる』って言うでしょ。

A: What good is it going to do me to put aside so little savings each time?
B: But remember the saying, ***"Mountains are made from grains of sand."***

Happoo Bijin

八方美人

67. "a beauty in eight directions"

(one who tries to please everyone, one who seeks popularity at the expense of integrity)

Happo means eight directions. *Bijin* literally means a beautiful woman. A person who wants to look attractive in eight different directions is a person trying too hard to please everyone, thus revealing a lack of integrity.

Sample text:
(Style: spoken/casual (blunt)/male)

A: *Akio no yatsu, kyooryoku shite kureru tte. Saisho wa iya da tte itta n da kedo sa.*
B: *Iya, aitsu wa **happoo bijin** da kara, ate ni naranai yo.*

A: 昭男のやつ、協力してくれるって。最初はいやだって言ったんだけどさ。
B: いや、あいつは八方美人だから、あてにならないよ。

A: Akio says he'll help us. He said he didn't want to at first, though.
B: Well, he's the type who ***tries to please everyone,*** so you really can't count on him.

Hito Hata Ageru

ひと旗あげる

"to hoist one's own flag"

(to succeed in business, particularly one's own enterprise)

In feudal times, conquering warriors would raise the flag of their lord on the battle site. Raising the flag in Japan today still symbolizes victory, particularly in reference to independent entrepreneurs who succeed in business after starting from scratch.

Sample text:
(Style: spoken/casual/A = female, B = male)

A: *Kawakami-san no musukosan, kondo jigyoo o hajimeru n desu tte.*

B: *Hoo, sorya taihen daroo na. Kono keiki ja, **hitohata ageru** no mo muzukashiku naru ippoo daroo kara naa.*

A: 川上さんの息子さん、今度事業をはじめるんですって。

B: ほう、そりゃ大変だろうな。この景気じゃ、**ひと旗あげ**るのもむずかしくなる一方だろうからなあ。

A: Did you know that Mr. Kawakami's son is launching a new business?

B: Is that right? It's going to be an uphill climb. **To succeed in your own enterprise** in today's business climate is getting harder and harder.

Hitori Zumoo o Toru

ひとり相撲を取る

"to wrestle a one-man *sumo*"

(to try hard at something without the support of others)

Obviously it takes two wrestlers to participate in a *sumo*
match. However enthusiastically one may wrestle with
oneself, the action itself will be incomplete. Therein lies the
off-on-one's-own (on a tangent) meaning of *hitori zumoo*.

Sample text:
(Style: spoken/casual/male)

A: *Rei no an, iinkai de teian shita n daroo?*
B: *Iya, sore ga ne, teian shita koto wa shita kedo **hitori
   zumoo o totta** kanji de dare mo shiji shite kurenakatta
   n da.*

A: 例の案、委員会で提案したんだろう？
B: いや、それがね、提案したことはしたけどひとり相撲を
   取った感じで誰も支持してくれなかったんだ。

A: You proposed that plan at the committee meeting,
   didn't you?
B: Yeah, I did. I proposed it, but it was **like wrestling a
   one-man sumo.** No one supported it.

Ishi no Ue ni mo Sannen

石の上にも三年

70.

"sitting on a stone for three years"

(perseverence wins in the end; endurance is a virtue.)

Japanese consider it a virtue to out-sit the competition. The common practice of making an investment, even at a loss, with the belief that a return will come *in the long run* comes from this simple, down-to-earth philosophy. Sitting on a rock for three years requires outrageous tenacity, but the longer you sit, the more secure you are in your position. And more to the point, you become the master of the situation because you have stuck with it. In fact, the cold ''stone'' may even seem warm and comfortable after three long years.

Sample text:
(Style: spoken/casual/A = female, B = male)

A: *Konna chiisana mise ja nakanaka okyakusan kisooni naishi, yappari dame kashira.*
B: *Sonna koto nai yo. Moo chotto jikan ga hitsuyoona n da yo.* **"Ishi no ue ni mo sannen"** *tte yuu daroo.*

A: こんな小さな店じゃなかなかお客さん来そうにないし、やっぱりだめかしら。
B: そんなことないよ。もうちょっと時間が必要なんだよ。『石の上にも三年』って言うだろう。

A: Customers just aren't coming to this small a shop. It may not work after all.
B: Nonsense. Give it time. You know what they say: **"Perseverence wins in the end."**

Juunin Toiro

十人十色

"ten people, ten colors"

(different strokes for different folks;
everyone has his or her own taste; "to
each his own")

Even though there is a large measure of truth to the
widespread belief that Japanese conform to the group, this
often-heard phrase attests to their awareness of the
differences in individual tastes.

Sample text:
(Style: spoken/casual/A = female, B = male)

A: *Kondo no paatii no ryoori wa nani o tanonda no?*
B: *Nanika ii mono to itte mo **juunin toiro** dakara,*
   nakanaka kimaranakute ne. De, kekkyoku iroiro
   torimazete tanomu koto ni shita n da yo.

A: 今度のパーティーの料理は何をたのんだの?
B: 何かいいものと言っても十人十色だから、なかなか決ま
   らなくてね。で、結局いろいろとりまぜてたのむことに
   したんだよ。

A: What kind of food did you order for the party?
B: Since **everybody has his or her own taste,** we had a
   hard time deciding, but we finally came up with a
   menu that offers a lot of variety.

Nimaijita o Tsukau
二枚舌を使う

150

"to use two tongues"

(to speak from both sides of the mouth, to speak with a forked tongue)

This expression refers to the practice of ''speaking out of both sides of the mouth''—shading the meaning of one's words to appeal to a particular person or group, while purposely giving a different impression to others. In Japan, as elsewhere, this practice (though common) is considered duplicitous and hypocritical.

Sample text:
(Style: spoken/casual/A = male, B = female)

A: *Iyaa, chigau naa. Kono aida no kaigi de wa sonna koto wa ittenakatta naa.*
B: *Soo kashira. Kyoo no ohanashi o sono mama tsutaeta dake da kedo.*
A: *Saikin, Mori-san **nimaijita o tsukau** yooni natte kita ne. Hanashi ga dondon kawaru n da kara tamannai yo.*

A: いやあ、ちがうなあ。この間の会議ではそんなことは言ってなかったなあ。
B: そうかしら。今日のお話をそのまま伝えただけだけど。
A: 最近、森さん**二枚舌を使う**ようになってきたね。話がどんどん変わるんだからたまんないよ。

A: No, that's not it. He didn't say that in the meeting the other day.
B: Really? I'm just reporting to you what he said to me today.
A: Mori has recently gotten into this habit of ***speaking from both sides of the mouth.*** His story changes from minute to minute; I can't stand it!

151

73.

Ni no Ashi o Fumu

二の足を踏む

TAP TAP

"to step twice in the same spot"

(to hesitate, to have second thoughts before taking an action)

To step twice in the same place is not to advance forward. Thus the meaning of hesitation before continuing on a presumed or planned course of action.

Sample text:
(Style: written/informal)

*Sasuga puro sukiiyaa no Hayashi-shi mo, sono yama no minami shamen o mite **ni no ashi o funda.** Totemo nami no sukiiyaa de wa suberesoomo nai kyuukooka ga, haruka kanata no tani made tsuzuiteiru no dearu.*

さすがプロ・スキーヤーの林氏も、その山の南斜面を見て二の足を踏んだ。とても並のスキーヤーではすべれそうもない急降下が、はるかかなたの谷まで続いているのである。

Even Hayashi, a professional skier, ***hesitated*** when he faced the southern slope of the mountain. The nose-diving slope continued all the way down into the valley. The average skier wouldn't even think about trying it.

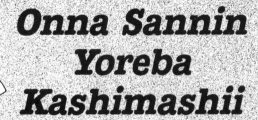

74

"Where three women gather, there is a noisy clamor."

(Women tend to talk a lot.)

The Chinese character for *kashimashii* ("clamorous") is made up of three small characters for "woman." In Japan it is understood that when two women get together, they tend to talk a lot. When three get together, it becomes *really* noisy.

Sample text:
(Style: spoken/casual/male)

A: *Tonari no heya, taihenna sawagashisa da.*
B: *Sorya soo daroo.* ***"Onna sannin yoreba kashimashii"*** *tte yuu noni, gonin atsumatte shabetteru n da kara ne.*

A: 隣の部屋、大変な騒がしさだ。
B: そりゃ、そうだろう。『女三人寄れば姦しい』って言うのに、五人集まってしゃべってるんだからね。

A: Such a racket they're making next door!
B: What do you expect? If it's true that **when three women gather there is a noisy clamor,** now you know what it sounds like when five of them get together.

Sannin Yoreba Monju no Chie

三人寄れば文珠の知恵

75

"Three people together have the wisdom of a Buddha."

(two heads are better than one)

Monju is the Saint of Wisdom in the Buddhist faith. Similar to *"two heads are better than one,"* the Japanese proverb suggests that even average people, when working in a group, can come up with a great idea.

Sample text:
(Style: spoken/casual/A = female, B = male)

A: *Kaigishitsu de nanika hisohiso hanashiteru kedo, nani shiteru no?*
B: *Kondo no purojekuto no gen'an o netteru rashii yo.*
A: *Daijoobu kashira. Demo, maa **"sannin yoreba Monju no chie"** tte yuu kara...*

A: 会議室で何かひそひそ話してるけど、何してるの?
B: こんどのプロジェクトの原案を練ってるらしいよ。
A: 大丈夫かしら。でも、まあ『三人寄れば文珠の知恵』って言うから…。

A: They're whispering among themselves in the meeting room; what are they up to?
B: They seem to be brainstorming on a new project.
A: Do you really think they can do it? Oh well, they say, ***"Two heads are better than one."***

Sushizume

すし詰め

"packed like *sushi*"

(very crowded, jam-packed)

This expression is similar in meaning to "packed like sardines." *Sushi*, the combination of raw fish with vinegared rice, is popular in Japan and increasingly so in the United States and Europe. Take-out *sushi* is often bought in little boxes called *sushi-ori*, in which the *sushi* pieces are packed tightly.

Sample text:
(Style: spoken/casual/male)

A: *Atarashii shigoto, tanoshii kedo, tsuukin ga taihen de ne. Maiasa* **sushizume** *no densha de ichijikan na n da yo.*
B: *Taihen da ne.*

A: 新しい仕事、楽しいけど、通勤が大変でね。毎朝すし詰めの電車で一時間なんだよ。
B: 大変だね。

A: My new job is a lot of fun, but commuting is terrible. Every morning I spend an hour in a **jam-packed** train!
B: That's awful!

Section Five

From Place to Place

77.
Ana ga Attara
Hairitai

穴があったら入りたい

"If there were a hole, I'd want to crawl into it."

("I'm so ashamed"; "I could've died of embarrassment.")

Sometimes your embarrassment is so acute you want to disappear completely from the scene. Unfortunately, in most cases you're stuck with braving it out. Yet were there a hole, you'd crawl into it.

Sample text:
(Style: written/informal)

*Paatii no sekijoo de kyuuni aisatsu o tanomare, taihen komatta koto ga aru. Ki ga dooten shiteita tame ka, jooshi no namae o machigaete itteshimai, hontooni **ana ga attara hairitai** kimochi datta. Yahari aisatsu o tanomu nara maemotte onegai shite moraereba arigatai mono da.*

パーティーの席上で急にあいさつをたのまれ、大変困ったことがある。気が動転していたためか、上司の名前をまちがえて言ってしまい、本当に穴があったら入りたい気持ちだった。やはり、あいさつをたのむなら前もってお願いしてもらえればありがたいものだ。

I was once in big trouble when asked without warning to give a speech at a party. I must have been upset; I used the wrong name in reference to my boss. ***I wanted to crawl into a hole!*** It is preferable to ask beforehand if you want someone to give a speech.

78.

Ishibashi o Tataite Wataru

石橋をたたいて渡る

TAP TAP

78. "to tap a stone bridge before crossing it"

(to proceed with caution, to test the waters before jumping in)

Even a bridge made of stone (which on the face of it is sturdier than a wooden bridge) needs to be tested before crossing. The English near-equivalent is "look before you leap."

Sample text:
(Style: spoken/casual/A = female, B = male)

A: *Watashi, doo shite mo kabuken te kau ki ni naranai no.*
B: *Sore mo ii daroo. **"Ishibashi o tataite wataru"** tte yuu kotoba mo aru n dashi. Chokin ja amari fuenai kedo, yoojin shita hoo ga anzen daroo na.*

A: 私、どうしても株券て買う気にならないの。
B: それもいいだろう。『石橋をたたいて渡る』っていう言葉もあるんだし。貯金じゃ余り増えないけど、用心した方が安全だろうな。

A: I simply don't feel like buying stocks.
B: That's OK. They say, ***"Tap a stone bridge before crossing it."*** Keeping your money in savings accounts won't accumulate much, but it's always safe to be cautious.

165

Kusawake

草分け

"parting the grass"

(pioneering, innovation, original thinking)

The phrase conjures up a man parting the tall grass with his hands. Metaphorically it means leading the way, going where no one has gone before, pioneering.

Sample text:
(Style: written/informal)

*Kare no onshi wa nihon ni okeru denshi koogaku no **kusawake** teki sonzai de, genzai katsuyakuchuu no gijutsusha o nannin mo sodateteiru.*

彼の恩師は日本における電子工学の**草分**け的存在で、現在活躍中の技術者を何人も育てている。

His teacher has led a ***pioneering*** life in the field of Japanese electronics and has educated many prominent engineers who are currently quite productive.

Onobori-san

おのぼりさん

80. "One who journeys to the capital"

(country bumpkin, hick, hayseed, someone from the sticks)

San in this phrase is the obligatory honorific that translates simply as "Mr." or "Ms." *Nobori* refers to heading toward the capital of Japan. With the addition of the honorific prefix *o-*, the phrase becomes a satirical reference to the stereotypical lack of sophistication of someone who has come from the "sticks."

Sample text:
(Style: spoken/casual/female)

A: *Kondo nyuusha shite kita Hara-san ne, chihoo no sanson kara jookyoo shite kita n da tte.*
B: *Aa, sore de na no ne. Ikanimo **onobori-san** tte kakkoo shiteru no wa.*

A: 今度入社してきた原さんね、地方の山村から上京して来たんだって。
B: ああ、それでなのね。いかにも**おのぼりさん**ってかっこうしてるのは。

A: You know the new employee, Ms. Hara? I hear she came to Tokyo from a small mountain village in the country.
B: Oh, that explains it. She certainly dresses like a **country bumpkin.**

169

Sumeba Miyako

住めば都

"Where one lives is the capital city."

(Wherever one lives, one comes to love it.)

Miyako means "the capital," but carries the connotation of the best place, the center of everything, the place to be. This short expression is similar in sentiment to "there's no place like home."

Sample text:
(Style: written/formal)

*Watashi wa saisho, Kyuushuu wa amari suki dewa arimasen deshita. Shikashi **sumeba miyako** to iwareru yooni, ima wa koko Kurume ga watashi no daini no furusato no yoona ki ga shiteimasu.*

私は最初、九州はあまり好きではありませんでした。しかし、住めば都と言われるように、今はここ久留米が私の第二のふるさとのような気がしています。

At first I didn't like Kyushu. But as the saying goes, ***"Wherever one lives, one comes to love it."*** Nowadays I feel as if Kurume is my second hometown.

Watari ni Fune

渡りに舟

"a boat to cross on"

(timely assistance, something that saves the day)

Poetically, "when you need to cross the river, luckily you find a boat to take you." The phrase means to "luck out." Used when something fortunate occurs when you need it most. A timely stroke of luck.

Sample text:
(Style: spoken/casual/female)

A: *Kodomo no mendoo o mite kureru hito o sagashiteta n da kedo, nakanaka ii hito ga inakute ne. Soshitara kyuuni tonari ni choodo ii hito ga utsutte kita no yo. Dooshiyoo ka to komatteita n da kedo, **watari ni fune** to wa kono koto ne.*

A: 子供のめんどうを見てくれる人をさがしてたんだけど、なかなかいい人がいなくてね。そしたら急に隣にちょうどいい人が移って来たのよ。どうしようかと困っていたんだけど、渡りに舟とはこのことね。

A: I was searching everywhere for someone who could look after my child, but I couldn't find anyone. Then all of a sudden the perfect person moved in next door! I was getting desperate, but she **saved the day!**

Section Six

More Cultural Keys

83. Asameshi Mae

朝飯前

"before the morning meal"

(a piece of cake, an easy task)

Meshi literally means cooked rice. The morning's cooked rice (breakfast) is the first source of energy for the day. A task that can be completed even before one's first meal is something requiring almost no effort.

Sample text:
(Style: spoken/casual/female)

A: *Kondo no koorasu no renshuu ne, yooji de derarenaku natta no. Kiyohara-san piano no bansoo hikiukete kureru kashira.*

B: *Daijoobu desho. Kitto hikiukete kureru n janai? Koorasu no bansoo nante kanojo ni totte wa, honno **asameshi mae** dashi ne.*

A: 今度のコーラスの練習ね、用事で出られなくなったの。清原さんピアノの伴奏引き受けてくれるかしら。

B: 大丈夫でしょ。きっと引き受けてくれるんじゃない? コーラスの伴奏なんて彼女にとっては、ほんの**朝飯前**だしね。

A: Something's come up, and I can't make the next chorus practice. I was wondering if Ms. Kiyohara would be willing to take over the piano accompaniment.

B: I'm sure she'll substitute for you, all right. For her, playing the accompaniment for the chorus is **a piece of cake.**

Baka wa Shinanakya Naoranai

ばかは死ななきゃ治らない

84. "Only death can cure a fool."

(Once a fool, always a fool.)

A derogatory term used in reference to someone who consistently demonstrates incompetence or poor judgment. Said in moments of exasperation, the phrase suggests an attitude of "I give up; there's no hope for you."

Sample text:
(Style: spoken/casual/male)

A: *Aitsu, hontooni zetsubooteki da ne. Nani yatte mo dame na n da.*
B: ***"Baka wa shinanakya naoranai"*** *tte ne. Ima sara kaeyoo to shite mo muri daroo.*

A: あいつ、本当に絶望的だね。何やってもダメなんだ。
B: 『ばかは死ななきゃ治らない』ってね。今さら変えようとしても無理だろう。

A: He's hopeless. That idiot can't do anything right.
B: Well, they say, ***"Only death can cure a fool."*** It's probably impossible to change him now.

Chan-Pon

ちゃんぽん

"ching-boom"

(a combination of ingredients [often that don't mix well], a medley of elements)

Chan is the sound of a chime, *pon*, the sound of a hand drum. When played simultaneously the result is a dissonant, jarring sound. *Chan-pon* is used to mean the result of mixing things together that should not be mixed, often with unfortunate consequences—whiskey and beer, spaghetti and Japanese *miso* soup.

Sample text:
(Style: spoken/casual/male)

A: *Kinoo wa doo shita no?*
B: *Sake to biiru o **chan-pon** ni nonda n de, hidoi futsuka yoi de sa. Totemo asa jogingu ni iku yoona jootai janakatta n da.*

A: きのうはどうしたの?
B: 酒とビールをちゃんぽんに飲んだんで、ひどい二日酔いでさ。とても朝ジョギングに行くような状態じゃなかったんだ。

A: What happened yesterday?
B: I **mixed** drinking sake and beer, and I got this terrible hangover. I was in no condition to go jogging in the morning.

Deru Kui wa Utareru

出る杭は打たれる

"The stake that sticks up will be pounded down."

(Excellence is shot down by mediocrity; doing better than others evokes jealousy; difference is forced into conformity.)

Commentary offered in explanation for why a gifted individual who may be head and shoulders above the norm is brought down to size by the members of his or her group. Quite literally, the stake that sticks out above the other stakes in a row is brought into line by being pounded down.

Sample text:
(Style: spoken/casual/male)

A: *Takahashi wa atarashii kaisha ni utsutta kedo umaku ikanai rashii na.*

B: *Aitsu, atama ga yosugiru n da. **"Deru kui wa utareru"** tte yuu daro. Sore ga tamaranai n janai ka, aitsu no koto da kara.*

A: 高橋は新しい会社に移ったけどうまくいかないらしいな。

B: あいつ、頭が良すぎるんだ。『出る杭は打たれる』って言うだろう。それがたまらないんじゃないか、あいつのことだから。

A: You know Takahashi, he moved to a new company, but he isn't getting along too well, I hear.

B: He's too brilliant. ***"Excellence is shot down by mediocrity,"*** you know. He probably can't stand it, knowing him.

Hakoiri Musume

箱入り娘

87. "a girl that's kept in a box"

(an innocent girl of a good family, an over-protected daughter)

A pre-war parlor game featured little wooden figures that were moved around (as in a board game). The figures represented members of a typical family and were kept stored in a box. The idealized *musume* (daughter) came to symbolize the shy, sheltered character of a girl who has never left home (the box). *Hakoiri musume* refers to an unworldly daughter from a good family.

Sample text:
(Style: spoken/formal/female)

A: *Kyooko-san, Amerika ni ryuugaku suru n desu tte.*
B: *Ara, sore, otoosan mo okaasan mo OK shita no? Anna **hakoiri musume** o Amerika ni dasu nante sazokashi shinpai deshoo nee.*

A: 京子さん、アメリカに留学するんですって。
B: あら、それ、お父さんもお母さんもOKしたの？　あんな箱入り娘をアメリカに出すなんてさぞかし心配でしょうねえ。

A: I hear Kyoko is going to the States to study.
B: Oh? Did her parents approve? They must be very concerned about sending such an **over-protected daughter** off all the way to the States.

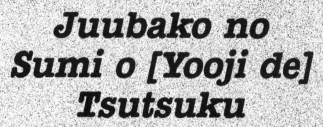

Juubako no Sumi o [Yooji de] Tsutsuku

重箱の隅を〔ようじで〕つつく

"to pick at the corners of a food-serving box [with a toothpick]"

(to be obsessively oriented toward inconsequential details, to dwell on minutiae, to split hairs)

Juubako is a box-shaped container for serving food. After the meal, one or two small pieces of food may remain stuck in the corners. Only an obsessive person would try to remove the left-over particles with a toothpick.

Sample text:
(Style: spoken/formal)

A: *Tashiro-san to no hanashi wa zenzen susumanai n desu yo ne.* **Juubako no sumi o tsutsuku** *yoona doo demo ii yoona hanashi bakari de, juudaina koto wa minna atomawashi. Kore ja itsu ni nattara saishuu kettei made motte ikeru mono yara . . .*
B: *Soo na n desu ka. Sore wa taihen desu ne.*

A: 田代さんとの話はぜんぜん進まないんですよね。**重箱の隅をつつく**ようなどうでもいいような話ばかりで、重大なことはみんなあとまわし。これじゃいつになったら最終決定までもっていけるものやら。
B: そうなんですか。それは大変ですね。

A: Talking with Mr. Tashiro never goes anywhere. He only **dwells on minutiae,** and important issues are left behind. I have no idea when the final decision will be made.
B: Is that so? Too bad.

Kataboo o Katsugu

片棒をかつぐ

"to shoulder one's end of the pole"

(to take part in, to hold up one's end of the operation, to have a hand in)

In feudal times, palanquin and coffin carriers worked in pairs. The responsibility for lifting and transporting was equally divided. To shoulder one's end of the pole means to hold up one's end of the operation, taking full responsibility for being an equal partner.

Sample text:
(Style: spoken/A = casual male, B = formal male)

A: *Iyaa, ano jiken wa jinjika no Yamada-san ga **kataboo o katsuida** rashii yo.*
B: *Yappari soo na n desu ka. Maa, Kawai-san hitori de, anna daisoreta koto o keikaku suru hazu wa nai to omottemashita ga ne.*

A: いやあ、あの事件は人事課の山田さんが**片棒**をかついだらしいよ。
B: やっぱりそうなんですか。まあ、川井さんひとりで、あんな大それたことを計画するはずはないと思ってましたがね。

A: Well, it appears that Mr. Yamada from the personnel department **had a hand in** that affair.
B: Just as I guessed. I figured that Mr. Kawai couldn't possibly have come up with such an ingenious plan all by himself.

Kooin Ya no Gotoshi

光陰矢のごとし

90. "Light and darkness fly like an arrow."

(Time flies; time and tide wait for no man.)

Koo means "light"; *in* means "shadow" or darkness." Together they refer to the passage of light into darkness (day and night)—in other words, time. The sentiment behind the phrase is close to "Life is short."

Sample text:
(Style: spoken/formal)

*Hayai mono de kono kaisha ni haitte kara sanjuunen no nengetsu ga tachimashita. **Kooin ya no gotoshi** to iwaremasu ga, watashi ni totte no kono sanjuunen wa amarini mijikakatta to yuu no ga jikkan desu.*

早いものでこの会社に入ってから、三十年の年月がたちました。『光陰矢のごとし』と言われますが、私にとってのこの三十年は余りに短かったというのが実感です。

It's been 30 short years since I joined this company. As the proverb ***"Time flies like an arrow"*** goes, my 30 years have been indeed too short.

91.
Koshikake
腰かけ

91. "a temporary sitting place"

(a stepping stone for something better, for the next stage)

It's an accepted custom that Japanese women office workers looking for husbands willingly accept menial jobs in corporations. Their position is seen as temporary. *Koshikake* means a chair, a bench, or a stool; an object upon which one rests briefly. It's easy to see how the phrase would come to mean a stepping stone to the next stage of life (most frequently wife and homemaker).

Sample text:
(Style: spoken/casual/female)

A: *Jinjika no Kanai-san, iyoiyo kekkon da tte.*
B: *Hee, yokatta wa ne. Doose* **koshikake** *de tsutometeta n da kara, hayaku aite ga mitsukatte.*

A: 人事課の金井さん、いよいよ結婚だって。
B: へーえ、良かったわね。どうせ腰かけで勤めてたんだから、早く相手がみつかって。

A: Did you hear Ms. Kanai is getting married?
B: Really? That's good. Her job here was only *a stepping stone* anyway. Good for her to have found someone to marry so quickly.

Kusai Mono ni wa Futa o Suru

臭いものにはふたをする

"to cover foul-smelling things"

(to opt for short-term solutions, to [temporarily] push aside and ignore problems)

Offenses to the nose are likely to command immediate attention. But simply to put a lid over the smell is not to make the source of the problem go away. Thus the meaning of a stop-gap or temporary fix.

Sample text:
(Style: written/informal)

*Ano hookoku de wa, konpontekina mondai ni genkyuu shiteinai. Yoosuruni **"kusai mono ni wa futa o suru"** to yuu hooshin na n daroo ga, mondai ga shinkokuka suru no wa, tannaru jikan no mondai to ieru.*

あの報告では、根本的な問題に言及していない。要するに『臭いものにはふたをする』という方針なんだろうが、問題が深刻化するのは、単なる時間の問題と言える。

That report completely glosses over the fundamental issues. In short, they are taking the position of **(temporarily) avoiding and ignoring the problem;** but it's merely a matter of time before the problem assumes serious proportions.

Madogiwa Zoku

窓際族

"the window tribe"

(people who have been promoted beyond function, people who have been "kicked upstairs")

The deeply entrenched seniority system of Japanese companies makes it difficult to rise to a top managerial position except after many years of service. Those who fail to attain a top position never enjoy the luxury of a private office, but they may be given a token reward of a desk next to the window in the large, open space where their juniors are also seated. The term "window tribe" refers to people who have been thus rewarded for their years of service but are out of the day-to-day running of the company.

Sample text:
(Style: spoken/casual/male)

A: *Yamakawa buchoo wa seki o utsutta no kai?*
B: *Aa, tonari no sekushon no oku no hoo e. Himitsu da kedo ne, kare **madogiwa zoku** no nakamairi shita n da.*

A: 山川部長は席を移ったのかい?
B: ああ、隣のセクションの奥の方へ。秘密だけどね、彼窓際族の仲間入りしたんだ。

A: Did Mr. Yamakawa, the manager, move?
B: Yeah, toward the back in the next section. It's supposed to be a secret, but he's been **kicked upstairs.**

Noren ni Udeoshi

のれんに腕押し

94. "to push against the entry curtain"

(a useless and completely ineffective action, a wasted effort)

When the *noren* (curtain with the store name printed on it) is hanging in the doorway of a noodle shop, Japanese restaurant, tea house, or other classically Japanese establishment, the place is "open for business." Since the *noren* is a hanging cloth, nothing is achieved by pushing one's arm against it. Such is the feeling one experiences when taking an action (through words or deeds) which elicits no response whatsoever.

Sample text:
(Style: spoken/casual/male)

A: *Dame da na, yappari. Are kore isshookenmei settoku shiyoo to shite mo hannoo nashi. Kore ja mattaku, **noren ni udeoshi** mo ii toko sa.*
B: *Yowatta ne.*

A: だめだな、やっぱり。あれこれ一生懸命説得しようとしても反応なし。これじゃ全く、のれんに腕押しもいいとこさ。
B: 弱ったね。

A: It's not working. I'm trying everything I can to convince him, but there's absolutely no response! It's **completely ineffective**...
B: Sorry to hear that.

Onaji Kama no Meshi o Kutta

同じ釜の飯を食った

95. "having eaten rice from the same pot"

(having shared a common experience, having been through a lot together)

Eating rice from the same pot is the Japanese equivalent of "breaking bread together." Communal eating establishes a sense of friendship and loyalty among those who literally eat out of the same pot. Most often used in reaffirming a special relationship developed through shared experiences.

Sample text:
(Style: spoken/casual/male)

A: *Doonika tanomu yo. **Onaji kama no meshi o kutta** naka daroo. Soo tsumetai koto o yuu na yo.*

A: どうにかたのむよ。同じ釜の飯を食った仲だろう。そう冷たいことを言うなよ。

A: Won't you do this for me? Haven't we **been through a lot together?** Don't disappoint me, huh.

Saji o Nageru

サジを投げる

96.

"to throw away the spoon"

(to give up in despair, to throw in the towel)

In ancient times the Japanese doctor or pharmacist was expected to concoct a special formula that would cure the patient. The pressure to find the correct mixture of ingredients was so great that many a doctor would hurl the measuring spoon into the air in despair. Metaphorically, *saji o nageru* means to give up out of frustration. Often the phrase is used as an admonishment not to give up.

Sample text:
(Style: written/informal)

Kyooikusha naru mono wa, donna gakusei ni taishite mo **saji o nagete** *wa naranai. Ningen wa dare de mo nanika no kakusareta sainoo ga aru mono da kara dearu.*

教育者なるものは、どんな学生に対しても**サジを投げて**はならない。人間は誰でも何かの隠された才能があるものだからである。

Educators must not **give up** on any student, for every human being has some ability yet to be tapped.

Sashimi no Tsuma

刺身のつま

"garnish for raw fish"

(insignificant participant, uninfluential presence)

However attractive, the garnish that accompanies a serving of *sashimi* is of no significance. Some people may not even notice its presence. Such is the degree of dismissal *sashimi no tsuma* carries when used in discounting the importance of a person's attendance at a meeting or gathering.

Sample text:
(Style: spoken/casual/female)

A: *Yuri-san to yuushoku ni iku yotei janakatta no?*
B: *Doose watashi ga shusseki shite mo **sashimi no tsuma** da kara dotchi; demo ii no yo.*

A: ゆりさんと夕食に行く予定じゃなかったの?
B: どうせ私が出席しても**刺身のつま**だからどっちでもいいのよ。

A: Weren't you supposed to go to a dinner party with Yuri?
B: Well, even if I attend, ***my presence there doesn't really matter,*** so it's not important if I go or not.

Sode no Shita

袖の下

98.

"under one's sleeve"

(under the table, off the books, bribery)

The large sleeve of the Japanese kimono makes for an ideal place to hide or to hand-off money. Today kimonos are seldom worn by Japanese men (and almost never when transacting business), but the phrase *sode no shita* is still very much in use. It has come to mean primarily some form of bribe.

Sample text:
(Style: spoken/casual/male)

A: *Naze anna an ga tootta n daroo.*
B: *Iinchoo ga **sode no shita** demo moratteru n daroo. Soo demo nakya tooru hazu nai yo.*

A: なぜあんな案が通ったんだろう。
B: 委員長が袖の下でももらってるんだろう。そうでもなきゃ通るはずないよ。

A: I wonder why that proposal passed.
B: Maybe the committee chairman was given some sort of **bribe.** Otherwise, it should never have passed.

Suna o Kamu Yoo

砂をかむよう

99.

"like chewing sand"

(dull, unhappy, and wearisome [life])

Most often used to describe a dull, uninteresting life. It's hard to imagine a more tasteless experience than having to eat (or chew) sand day in and day out. The phrase connotes a dull, bad-tasting, and unhappy life.

Sample text:
(Style: written/informal)

*Hannin wa tsuma o koroshite kara gonenkan, tokai no katasumi de tooboo seikatsu o okutta. Jikyoo ni yoruto, seishinteki ni mo busshitsuteki ni mo kurushiku, shakai kara koritsu shiteita tame, mainichi ga ajike naku, masani **suna o kamu yoona** seikatsu datta to yuu.*

犯人は妻を殺してから五年間、都会の片すみで逃亡生活を送った。自供によると、精神的にも物質的にも苦しく、社会から孤立していたため、毎日が味気なく、まさに砂をかむような生活だったと言う。

The murderer, after killing his wife, spent five years as a fugitive. According to his confession, he suffered both mentally and materially and, living isolated from society, he led a ***dull, unhappy, and wearisome*** life.

Taikoban o Osu

太鼓判を押す

"to stamp a drum-size seal"

(to vouch enthusiastically for a person, to recommend highly, virtually to guarantee a person's success)

On official documents in Japan, a name-stamp is used rather than a signature. Seals vary in size and shape, but generally the bigger the seal, the greater the status. The seal for a university, for example, will be larger and more impressive-looking than the seal for an individual. Metaphorically, a ''drum-size seal'' is an enthusiastic endorsement, often used as a strong recommendation.

Sample text:
(Style: spoken/formal/male)

A: *Aa, Kawakami ga otaku no kaisha ni nyuusha shita n desu ka. Kare wa yuushuu deshite ne. Hitogara wa watashi ga **taikoban o oshimasu** yo.*

A: ああ、川上がおたくの会社に入社したんですか。彼は優秀でしてね。人柄は私が**太鼓判を押**しますよ。

A: Oh, Kawakami is now at your company? He's brilliant, isn't he? And I can **highly recommend** his personality, too.

Yuushuu no Bi o Kazaru

有終の美を飾る

101. "to decorate the ending with beauty"

(to achieve something great just before the end [of one's career], to end with a flourish, to go out with a bang)

Equivalent to the positive tone of "ending on a high note," this expression refers to getting a well-deserved bump of recognition immediately before ending one's career.

Sample text:
(Style: spoken/formal)

*Kawamura sensei wa sanjuugonenkan ni watari, kyooiku hitosuji ni doryoku shite korare mashita ga, kondo zannenni mo taishoku nasaru koto ni narimashita. Sakunendo wa honkoo ga ongaku konkuuru de ken daiichii ni narimashita ga, kore wa hitoeni Kawamura sensei no go-shidoo ni yoru mono deshita. Masani **yuushuu no bi o kazatte** kudasatta wake de arimasu.*

川村先生は三十五年間に渡り、教育一筋に努力してこられましたが、こん度残念にも退職なさることになりました。昨年度は本校が音楽コンクールで県第一位になりましたが、これはひとえに川村先生の御指導によるものでした。正に有終の美を飾ってくださったわけであります。

Mr. Kawamura has for 35 years dedicated himself to education, and now we are all sorry to learn that he is retiring. Last year our school ranked first in the prefectural music contest; this was all possible only because of his leadership. He certainly has **ended** his career **with a flourish.**

Index of Idioms by Key Images

(Numbers correspond to idiom numbers.)

Arm
Ude o Migaku 63
Noren ni Udeoshi 94
Arrow
Kooin Ya no Gotoshi 90

Badger
Onaji Ana no Mujina 32
Bamboo
Take o Watta Yoo 13
Belly
Haragei 53
Bird
Ashimoto kara Tori ga Tatsu 25
Hane o Nobasu 26
Tatsu Tori Ato o Nigosazu 34
Bird, crane
Tsuru no Hitokoe 35
Bird, sparrow
Suzume no Namida 33
Blossom
Hana ni Arashi 2
Hana yori Dango 3
Iwanu ga Hana 5
Boat
Watari ni Fune 82
Body, parts of (see each part entry)
Bone
Uma no Hone 36
Box
Hakoiri Musume 87
Box, food serving
Juubako no Sumi o [Yooji de] Tsutsuku 88
Breakfast
Asameshi Mae 83
Breath
Mushi no Iki 43

Capital
Onobori-san 80
Sumeba Miyako 81
Cat
Karite Kita Neko no Yoo 27
Neko mo Shakushi mo 28
Neko ni Koban 29
Neko no Hitai 30
Neko no Te mo Karitai 31
Cherry
Sakura 10
Cloud
Kumo o Tsukamu Yoo 19
Crying
Nakitsura ni Hachi 44
Cucumber
Uri Futatsu 14

Daughter
Hakoiri Musume 87
Dust
Chiri mo Tsumoreba Yama to Naru 66

Ear
Mimi ga Itai 58
End(ing)
Tatsu Tori Ato o Nigosazu 34
Yuushuu no Bi o Kazaru 101
Eye
Shiroi me de Miru 61

Face
Abata mo Ekubo 47
Fish
Gomame no Hagishiri 37
Manaita no Ue no Koi 42
Saba o Yomu 45
Frog
I no Naka no Kawazu [Taikai o Shirazu] 40

Head
Atama ga Sagaru 51
Heart
Ishin Denshin 54
Shinzoo ga Tsuyoi 60
Hole
Ana ga Attara Hairitai 77
Onaji Ana no Mujina 32
Horse
Uma no Hone 36

Insect
Mushi no Iki 43
Tade Kuu Mushi mo Sukizuki 46
Insect, bee
Hachi no Su o Tsutsuita Yoo 38
Nakitsura ni Hachi 44
Insect, mosquito
Ka no Naku Yoona Koe 41

Japanese dish
Sashimi no Tsuma 97
Sushizume 76
Leaf
Ne mo Ha mo Nai 9
Leg
Agura o Kaku 48
Ashimoto kara Tori ga Tatsu 25
Ashimoto o Miru 49
Ashi o Arau 50
Ni no Ashi o Fumu 73
Letter
Kaze no Tayori 18

Medicine
Ryooyaku Kuchi ni Nigashi   59
Moss
Korogaru Ishi ni Koke Musazu   6
Mountain
Chiri mo Tsumoreba Yama
to Naru   66
Mountain, peak of
Takane no Hana   12
Music
Chan-pon   85

Noisy
Hachi no Su o Tsutsuita Yoo   38
Onna Sannin Yoreba Kashimashii   74

One
Hito Hata Ageru   68
Hitori Zumoo o Toru   69
Tsuru no Hitokoe   35
Octopus
Hippari Dako   39

Palanquin
Ashimoto o Miru   49
Kataboo o Katsugu   89
Pepper
Sanshoo wa Kotsubu de mo
[Piririto] Karai   11
Pole
Kataboo o Katsugu   89

Rain
Ame ga Furoo to Yari ga Furoo
to   16
Ame Futte Ji Katamaru   17
Rice, cooked
Asameshi Mae   83
Onaji Kama no Meshi o Kutta   95
Rice, plant of
Minoru hodo Atama no Sagaru
Inaho Kana   7
Rice ladles
Neko mo Shakushi mo   28
Root
Nemawashi   8
Ne mo Ha mo Nai   9

Saying
Iwanu ga Hana   5
Seal
Taikoban o Osu   100
Sesame
Gomasuri   1
Shoulder
Katami ga Semai   56
Sign, hanging cloth
Noren ni Udeoshi   94
Sitting place
Koshikake   91
Sleeve
Sode no Shita   98
Smell
Kusai Mono ni wa Futa o Suru   92

Spear
Ame ga Furoo to Yari ga Furoo
to   16
Spoon
Saji o Nageru   96
Stake
Deru Kui wa Utareru   86
Stone
Ishi no Ue ni mo Sannen   70
Korogaru Ishi ni Koke Musazu   6
Stone bridge
Ishibashi o Tataite Wataru   78
Storm
Hana ni Arashi   2
Sumo
Hitori Zumoo o Toru   69
Sushi
Sushizume   76
Sweets
Hana yori Dango   3

Tears
Suzume no Namida   33
Ten
Juunin Toiro   71
Three
Ishi no Ue ni mo Sannen   70
Onna Sannin Yoreba
Kashimashii   74
Sannin Yoreba Monju no Chie   75
Time
Kooin Ya no Gotoshi   90
Tongue
Nimaijita o Tsukau   72
Tree
Ne mo Ha mo Nai   9
Yoraba Taiju no Kage   15
Tree, root of
Nemawashi   8
Two
Uri Futatsu   14
Nimaijita o Tsukau   72
Ni no Ashi o Fumu   73

Waist
Koshi ga Hikui   57
Water
Mizu ni Nagasu   20
Mizu no Awa   21
Mizu o Utta Yoo   22
Mizu Shoobai   23
Yakeishi ni Mizu   24
Wind
Hana ni Arashi   2
Kaze no Tayori   18
Window
Madogiwa Zoku   93
Wing
Hane o Nobasu   26
Woman
Happoo Bijin   67
Onna Sannin Yoreba
Kashimashii   74

Index of Idioms Listed Alphabetically

(Numbers correspond to idiom numbers.)

Abata mo Ekubo 47
Agura o Kaku 48
Ame ga Furoo to Yari ga Furoo
  to 16
Ame Futte Ji Katamaru 17
Ana ga Attara Hairitai 77
Asameshi Mae 83
Ashimoto kara Tori ga Tatsu 25
Ashimoto o Miru 49
Ashi o Arau 50
Atama ga Sagaru 51
Awaseru Kao ga Nai 52

Baka wa Shinanakya
  Naoranai 84

Chan-Pon 85
Chiri mo Tsumoreba Yama to
  Naru 66

Deru Kui wa Utareru 86

Gomasuri 1
Gomame no Hagishiri 37

Hachi no Su o Tsutsuita Yoo 38
Hakoiri Musume 87
Hana ni Arashi 2
Hana yori Dango 3
Hane o Nobasu 26
Haragei 53
Happoo Bijin 67
Hippari Dako 39
Hito Hata Ageru 68
Hitori Zumoo o Toru 69

Imo (no Ko) o Arau Yoo 4
I no Naka no Kawazu [Taikai o
  Shirazu] 40
Ishibashi o Tataite Wataru 78
Ishin Denshin 54
Ishi no Ue ni mo Sannen 70
Iwanu ga Hana 5

Juubako no Sumi o [Yooji de]
  Tsutsuku 88
Juunin Toiro 71

Ka no Naku Yoona Koe 41
Kao ga Hiroi 55
Karite Kita Neko no Yoo 27
Kataboo o Katsugu 89
Katami ga Semai 56
Kaze no Tayori 18
Kooin Ya no Gotoshi 90
Korogaru Ishi ni Koke Musazu 6
Koshikake 91
Koshi ga Hikui 57

Kumo o Tsukamu Yoo 19
Kusai Mono ni wa Futa o
  Suru 92
Kusawake 79

Madogiwa Zoku 93
Manaita no Ue no Koi 42
Mimi ga Itai 58
Minoru hodo Atama no Sagaru
  Inaho Kana 7
Mizu ni Nagasu 20
Mizu no Awa 21
Mizu o Utta Yoo 22
Mizu Shoobai 23
Mushi no Iki 43

Nakitsura ni Hachi 44
Neko mo Shakushi mo 28
Neko ni Koban 29
Neko no Hitai 30
Neko no Te mo Karitai 31
Nemawashi 8
Ne mo Ha mo Nai 9
Nimaijita o Tsukau 72
Ni no Ashi o Fumu 73
Noren ni Udeoshi 94

Onaji Ana no Mujina 32
Onaji Kama no Meshi o
  Kutta 95
Onna Sannin Yoreba
  Kashimashii 74
Onobori-san 80

Ryooyaku Kuchi ni Nigashi 59

Saba o Yomu 45
Saji o Nageru 96
Sakura 10
Sannin Yoreba Monju no
  Chie 75
Sanshoo wa Kotsubu de mo
  [Piririto] Karai 11
Sashimi no Tsuma 97
Shinzoo ga Tsuyoi 60
Shiroi Me de Miru 61
Sode no Shita 98
Sumeba Miyako 81
Suna o Kamu Yoo 99
Sushizume 76
Suzume no Namida 33

Tade Kuu Mushi mo Sukizuki 46
Taikoban o Osu 100
Takane no Hana 12
Take o Watta Yoo 13
Tatsu Tori Ato o Nigosazu 34

Tsura no Kawa ga Atsui 62
Tsuru no Hitokoe 35

Ude o Migaku 63
Uma no Hone 36
Uri Futatsu 14
Ushirogami o Hikareru Omoi 64
Ushiroyubi o Sasareru Yoo 65

Watari ni Fune 82
Yakeishi ni Mizu 24
Yoraba Taiju no Kage 15
Yuushuu no Bi o Kazaru 101